OCT 0 8 2012

S0-ATF-903

Biography Today

*Profiles
of People
of Interest
to Young
Readers*

Volume 21
Issue 3
September 2012

Cherie D. Abbey
Managing Editor

*155 West Congress, Suite 200
Detroit, MI 48226*

Cherie D. Abbey, *Managing Editor*

Peggy Daniels, Laurie DiMauro, Jeff Hill, Kevin Hillstrom,
Laurie Hillstrom, and Diane Telgen, *Sketch Writers*

Allison A. Beckett and Mary Butler, *Research Staff*

* * *

Peter E. Ruffner, *Publisher*
Matthew P. Barbour, *Senior Vice President*

* * *

Elizabeth Collins, *Research and Permissions Coordinator*
Kevin M. Hayes, *Operations Manager*

Shirley Amore, Joseph Harris, Martha Johns,
and Kirk Kauffmann, *Administrative Staff*

Special thanks to Frederick G. Ruffner for creating this series.

Copyright © 2012 EBSCO Publishing, Inc.
ISSN 1058-2347 • ISBN 978-0-7808-1255-0

Library of Congress Cataloging-in-Publication Data

All rights reserved. No part of this publication may be reproduced or transmitted in any form or by any means, electronic or mechanical, including photocopy, recording, or any information storage and retrieval system, without permission in writing from the publisher.

The information in this publication was compiled from sources cited and from sources considered reliable. While every possible effort has been made to ensure reliability, the publisher will not assume liability for damages caused by inaccuracies in the data, and makes no warranty, express or implied, on the accuracy of the information contained herein.

This book is printed on acid-free paper meeting the ANSI Z39.48 Standard. The infinity symbol that appears above indicates that the paper in this book meets that standard.

Printed in the United States

Contents

Preface

Biography Today is a magazine designed and written for the young reader—ages 9 and above—and covers individuals that librarians and teachers tell us that young people want to know about most: entertainers, athletes, writers, illustrators, cartoonists, and political leaders.

The Plan of the Work

The publication was especially created to appeal to young readers in a format they can enjoy reading and readily understand. Each issue contains approximately 10 sketches arranged alphabetically. Each entry provides at least one picture of the individual profiled, and boldfaced rubrics lead the reader to information on birth, youth, early memories, education, first jobs, marriage and family, career highlights, memorable experiences, hobbies, and honors and awards. Each of the entries ends with a list of easily accessible sources designed to lead the student to further reading on the individual and a current address. Retrospective entries are also included, written to provide a perspective on the individual's entire career.

Biographies are prepared by Omnigraphics editors after extensive research, utilizing the most current materials available. Those sources that are generally available to students appear in the list of further reading at the end of the sketch.

Indexes

Cumulative indexes are an important component of *Biography Today*. Each issue of the *Biography Today* General Series includes a Cumulative Names Index, which comprises all individuals profiled in *Biography Today* since the series began in 1992. In addition, we compile three other indexes: the Cumulative General Index, Places of Birth Index, and Birthday Index. See our web site, www.biographytoday.com, for these three indexes, along with the Names Index. All *Biography Today* indexes are cumulative, including all individuals profiled in both the General Series and the Subject Series.

Our Advisors

This series was reviewed by an Advisory Board comprising librarians, children's literature specialists, and reading instructors to ensure that the concept of this publication—to provide a readable and accessible biographical magazine for young readers—was on target. They evaluated the title as it developed, and their suggestions have proved invaluable. Any errors, however, are ours alone. We'd like to list the Advisory Board members and to thank them for their efforts.

Gail Beaver
Adjunct Lecturer
University of Michigan
Ann Arbor, MI

Cindy Cares
Youth Services Librarian
Southfield Public Library
Southfield, MI

Carol A. Doll
School of Information Science and Policy
University of Albany, SUNY
Albany, NY

Kathleen Hayes-Parvin
Language Arts Teacher
Birney Middle School
Southfield, MI

Karen Imarisio
Assistant Head of Adult Services
Bloomfield Twp. Public Library
Bloomfield Hills, MI

Rosemary Orlando
Director
St. Clair Shores Public Library
St. Clair Shores, MI

Our Advisory Board stressed to us that we should not shy away from controversial or unconventional people in our profiles, and we have tried to follow their advice. The Advisory Board also mentioned that the sketches might be useful in reluctant reader and adult literacy programs, and we would value any comments librarians might have about the suitability of our magazine for those purposes.

Your Comments Are Welcome

Our goal is to be accurate and up to date, to give young readers information they can learn from and enjoy. Now we want to know what you think. Take a look at this issue of *Biography Today*, on approval. Contact me with your comments. We want to provide an excellent source of biographical information for young people. Let us know how you think we're doing.

Cherie Abbey
Managing Editor, *Biography Today*
Omnigraphics, Inc.
155 W. Congress, Suite 200
Detroit, MI 48226
www.omnigraphics.com
editorial@omnigraphics.com

Congratulations!

Congratulations to the following individuals and libraries who are receiving a free copy of *Biography Today*, Vol. 21, No. 3, for suggesting people who appear in this issue.

James P. Hibler, Kalkaska County Library, Grand Rapids, MI

Beth E. Meier, Hayward Middle School Library, Springfield, OH

Vicki Reutter, Cazenovia Junior-Senior High School, Cazenovia, NY

Yvette and Marjorie Shanks, O'Fallon, MO

Carol Starr, Sarah Banks Middle School, Wixom, MI

Shreya Subramanian, Troy, MI

Sharon Thackston, Gallatin Public Library, Gallatin, TN

Sierra M. Yoder, Shipshewana, IN

Alejandro Z., Mid-Valley Regional Branch Library, North Hills, CA

Judy Blume 1938-

American Author of Juvenile, Young Adult, and Adult Fiction

Award-Winning Writer of the Best-Selling Books *Are You There God? It's Me, Margaret*, *Deenie*, *Blubber*, *Forever*, *Tiger Eyes*, the *Fudge* Series, and Many More

BIRTH

Judy Blume (born Judy Sussman) was born on February 12, 1938, in Elizabeth, New Jersey. Her father, Rudolph Sussman, was a dentist. Her mother, Esther Sussman, was a homemaker. She has one older brother, named David.

YOUTH

Blume grew up in Elizabeth, New Jersey. She described herself as a shy, quiet, and anxious child. She was very close to her father, who was known for his warm, outgoing personality. "My father was fun. Everybody loved him.… He taught me about classical music."

As a child, Blume liked going to the movies, listening to the radio, and roller skating. She also liked dancing, singing, and painting. But reading books was her favorite thing to do, and she loved visiting the public library. "I not only liked the pictures and the stories but the feel and the smell of the books themselves. My favorite book was *Madeline* by Ludwig Bemelmans. I loved that book! I loved it so much I hid it in my kitchen toy drawer so my mother wouldn't be able to return it to the library.… I thought the copy I had hidden was the only copy in the whole world. I knew it was wrong to hide the book but there was no way I was going to part with *Madeline*," Blume said. "When I was older I liked the Betsy-Tacy books by Maud Hart Lovelace, and the Oz Books, and Nancy Drew mysteries. But I didn't find real satisfaction in reading until I was older. Because there weren't any books with characters who felt the way I did, who acted the way I did, with whom I could identify. I think I write the kinds of books I would have liked to read when young."

——— **"** ———

"My favorite book was Madeline *by Ludwig Bemelmans," Blume recalled. "I loved that book! I loved it so much I hid it in my kitchen toy drawer so my mother wouldn't be able to return it to the library.… I thought the copy I had hidden was the only copy in the whole world. I knew it was wrong to hide the book but there was no way I was going to part with* Madeline.*"*

——— **"** ———

Blume was also very imaginative. "I was a great pretender, always making up stories inside my head … but I never told anyone." Though she loved reading and making up her own stories, Blume did not think about becoming a writer. "When I was growing up, I dreamed about becoming a cowgirl, a detective, a spy, a great actress, or a ballerina," she explained. "I never really thought of writing professionally. I never knew it was a possibility."

During her childhood, Blume and her mother and brother lived for two years in Miami Beach, Florida. They moved there in the hope that the

Blume at a book signing with some of her fans.

warm climate would improve her brother's health. They lived with Blume's grandmother, while her father stayed in New Jersey. "As much as I missed my father, I loved it there. I played outside until dark. I was coming out of my shell. When I got back to New Jersey, I was a changed person, much more social."

As a teenager, Blume struggled with the social and emotional challenges of adolescence. She recalled being confused about her changing body and tumultuous feelings. "My father delivered these little lectures to me, the last one when I was 10, on how babies are made. But questions about what I was feeling, and how my body could feel, I *never* asked my parents," she said. "We kept our feelings to ourselves."

EDUCATION

Blume attended public schools in Elizabeth and Miami Beach. She was a good student and liked English and journalism classes the best. She was an editor of the school newspaper, sang in the chorus, and studied dance. Blume graduated with honors from Battin High School in Elizabeth, New Jersey.

After high school, Blume enrolled in Boston University. Only two weeks into her first year, she was diagnosed with mononucleosis and had to leave school. (Mononucleosis is an infectious disease that can cause fever, aches and pains, and tiredness. In extreme cases, it can take several months to recover from mono.) Blume enrolled in New York University the following year. She earned a bachelor's degree in early childhood education in 1961.

CAREER HIGHLIGHTS

Blume is widely recognized as one of the most popular and successful authors of fiction for children and young adults. Over the course of her long career, she has published more than 25 books. She has written picture books for very young children, chapter books for beginning readers, and novels for middle-grade readers, teens, and adults. Early in her career, Blume gained a reputation for being unafraid to tackle difficult and often taboo subjects like puberty, teenage sex, peer pressure, bullying, sibling rivalry, divorce, illness, and death.

Blume's readers often identify with the characters in her books, who face common issues like clueless parents, annoying siblings, problems at school, and feeling that they don't fit in. As a result, her books have remained extremely popular for generations of readers. Her books have been translated into 31 different languages; more than 80 million copies have been sold around the world; and 14 of her books are on the *Publishers Weekly* list of the all-time best-selling children's books.

Becoming a Writer

Blume described her decision to write books for young people as an accident. "My kids were about three and five and I wanted to do something, but I didn't want to go back to classroom teaching, which is what I was qualified for. I read my kids a lot of books, and I guess I just decided—Well, I could do that too. So when I washed the dinner dishes at night I would do imitation Dr. Seuss rhyming books; and each night by the time I'd done the dishes I would have a whole book. I would send some of them in to publishers and they would be rejected. They were terrible. That's how I started."

After two years of publishers' rejections, Blume enrolled in a graduate course at New York University on writing for young people. She enjoyed the class so much she took it twice. During this time, she published some short stories and finished the first draft of *The One in the Middle Is the Green Kangaroo*. This picture book for young children told the story of a middle child who feels left out of the family. In 1969, *The One in the Middle Is the Green Kangaroo* became Blume's first published book. She remembered her reaction to the news that it was going to be published as "overjoyed, hysterical, unbelieving! I felt like such a celebrity."

Writing for Middle-Grade Readers

Some of Blume's most popular books describe the everyday problems, struggles, and concerns of upper elementary and middle school readers. "The child from 9 to 12 interests me very much," she offered. "And so, those were the years that I like to write about." Her books for this age group focus on the experiences of growing up, including everyday problems and challenges often faced by many readers.

In 1970, Blume published *Iggie's House*, her first book for middle-grade readers. "*Iggie's House* was my first long book. I wrote it week by week, a chapter at a time, while taking a writing course at NYU," she said. *Iggie's House* tells the story of the racial tension surrounding the arrival of the Garbers, the first African-American family to move into an all-white neighborhood. Sixth-grader Winnie quickly becomes friends with the Garber children. But Winnie soon discovers that not everyone in the neighborhood shares her excitement to have new neighbors. Conflict grows as some of the long-time residents try to pressure the Garbers to leave the neighborhood. Winnie struggles to understand why some people seem to hate the Garbers without knowing anything about the family. As events unfold, Winnie learns about the lasting effects of racism on a community.

> "
>
> *"Margaret is fiction, but based on the kind of 12-year-old I was," Blume said about the book* Are You There God? It's Me, Margaret. *"Sitting down to write Margaret was just remembering what it was like for me, when I was Margaret's age. And you know, yeah for a while in my life I was totally obsessed by breast development and the idea of getting my period. And maybe that's because I was the late bloomer. I was sick of being the smallest in the class and the skinniest."*
>
> ""

Are You There God? It's Me, Margaret

In 1970, Blume also published *Are You There God? It's Me, Margaret,* the book that launched her reputation for creating frank stories about everyday concerns for kids. The story begins as 12-year-old Margaret's family moves from the city to the suburbs, where she will have to start sixth grade in a new school. Margaret is worried about being accepted in the new

JUDY BLUME

Are You There God? It's Me, Margaret
was Blume's first major novel for young readers.

neighborhood and making new friends. She is preoccupied with her own physical development and getting her first period. Margaret is also struggling with a crisis of religious identity—her mother is Christian and her father is Jewish. Confused about where she belongs, Margaret decides to visit as many different places of worship as she can in order to discover where she fits in.

Are You There God? It's Me, Margaret is regarded as a revolutionary and pioneering book because of its honest handling of the real-life concerns of pre-teen girls. It was first published during a time when books for young readers simply did not take on such taboo subjects as puberty, young girls getting their first period, and buying training bras. The book's realism and honesty won fans among critics and young readers. *Publishers Weekly* noted, "With sensitivity and humor Judy Blume has captured the joys, fears, and uncertainty that surround a young girl approaching adolescence." *New York Times Book Review* critic Dorothy Broderick called *Are You There God? It's Me, Margaret* "a warm, funny, and loving book, one that captures the essence of adolescence." The book became an instant phenomenon among young readers, particularly with girls around Margaret's age. Soon after its publication, Blume began receiving thousands of letters from readers who told her that Margaret's story was just like their own lives. "Margaret brought me my first and most loyal readers. I love her for that," Blume said.

"Margaret is fiction, but based on the kind of 12-year-old I was. Growing up, we did have a club like The PTSs [Pre-Teen Sensations]. And Margaret's interests and concerns were similar to mine. I was small and thin when thin wasn't in. I was a late developer and was anxious to grow like my friends. Margaret was right from my own sixth grade experience. I wanted to tell the truth as I knew it," Blume said. "Sitting down to write Margaret was just remembering what it was like for me, when I was Margaret's age. And you know, yeah for a while in my life I was totally obsessed by breast development and the idea of getting my period. And maybe that's because I was the late bloomer. I was sick of being the smallest in the class and the skinniest."

Are You There God? It's Me, Margaret is also noteworthy because of its direct handling of religious conflict during a time when religion defined social life in many communities. In the book, all of Margaret's friends belong to either a church or a synagogue. Her family doesn't observe any religion, so she belongs to neither. In *The Half-Jewish Book*, Daniel M. Klein and Freke Vuijst write, "The book actually talked frankly about young girls getting their first period! And about their fervent desire to start growing breasts!

So much did these shocking topics dominate discussions of this novel for children between 10 and 12 that hardly anything was said about the title character's perplexity concerning religious identity—a theme that runs through the book as dominantly as matters of maturing bodies do." As Blume observed, "I thought I was writing about organized religion, yet the book has become famous for dealing with puberty. Hardly anyone ever mentions religion or Margaret's very personal relationship with God."

More Books for Middle-Grade Readers

Blume's next book, *Then Again, Maybe I Won't,* was published in 1971. It tells the story of 12-year-old Tony, whose family is suddenly rich from the sale of his dad's new invention. Tony's family moves to a big house in a new neighborhood, and his life is turned upside down. People in the new neighborhood are very different from their old neighbors. His father sells the family's truck because the neighbors make comments about it being parked in their driveway. His mother lets the neighbors call her "Carol"because her real name—Carmella—is too hard to remember. Meanwhile, Tony's grandmother is acting strangely and refusing to come out of her room. As the story unfolds, Tony must face the challenges of his new school, a friend's shoplifting habit, and his own confusion over the sexual dreams he's begun to have almost every night. The book was another sensational success with young readers and critics alike. The *New York Times Book Review* noted, "Judy Blume is on target. Her understanding of young people is sympathetic and psychologically sound; her skill engages the reader in human drama."

In 1972, Blume published *It's Not the End of the World.* In this book, 12-year-old Karen must work through her emotions and navigate changes at home as her parents get divorced. Her parents fight all the time, but Karen thinks she can save their marriage. She tries plan after plan but nothing seems to work—her parents are still splitting up. The situation gets worse when her brother runs away, and again when Karen finds out she's moving to a new place with her mother and siblings. Karen has no choice but to find a way to adjust to it all.

At the time it was published, *It's Not the End of the World* was one of the first books for young readers that focused on the painful topic of divorce and its effect on children. By writing honestly about Karen's experiences, Blume once again gave voice to the fears and concerns of many young readers. *It's Not the End of the World* was praised by *Horn Book Magazine* as "A brisk, first-person narrative [that] believably delineates the bewilderment and anxiety affecting children of about-to-be-divorced parents.

JUDY BLUME

It's Not the End of the World
was one of the first books for young adults to deal with the topic of divorce.

Honest, but not depressing, [the book] explores with precision and sympathy the distinctive personality of a 12-year-old."

Blume's next book, *Deenie,* was published in 1973. This book tells the story of Deenie, a beautiful 13-year-old girl who is on her way to a modeling career at the insistence of her mother. Deenie's life changes forever when she is diagnosed with scoliosis, a condition in which a person's spine is curved from side to side. Deenie learns that she must wear a metal body brace that stretches from her neck to her hips. She will have to wear the brace almost all the time for the next four years. Her ability to move her body will be severely restricted, and her modeling career is over before it even begins. As Deenie learns to accept her situation, her sister and parents must also come to terms with changes in their lives.

According to Blume, Deenie and her story were based on a family she knew. "I met a lively 14-year-old girl with scoliosis. She seemed to be adjusting well to her condition and her brace but her mother was in tears over the situation,"Blume confided. "The basic idea for the book came from that meeting. Everything else about the family is fiction. I set the book in the town where I grew up—Elizabeth, New Jersey—and sent Deenie and her friends to my junior high school. I think of the story as one about parental expectations. Deenie's mother says: *Deenie's the beauty, Helen's the brain.* What happens when a parent pigeon-holes her children that way?"

Blubber, published in 1974, focuses on the effects of bullying. The story is told from the point of view of Jill, a fifth-grader who joins several classmates in the merciless and cruel bullying of Linda, an overweight and awkward girl. Jill finds it amusing to come up with new ways to be cruel to Linda. But as the story unfolds, an unexpected turn of events changes things for Jill. As she tries to resolve her own problems at school, Jill learns some important lessons about how to treat others.

Blubber became an immediate success with young readers as well as book reviewers. "Some adults are bothered by the language and the cruelty, but the kids get it. They live it," a reviewer observed in *School Library Journal.* "This is an accurate, entertaining, warts-and-all picture of under-12 social dynamics." Since its publication, the story has remained relevant and continues to affect readers. One fan is Diablo Cody, the author of the screenplays for the movies *Juno* and *Young Adult.* As she commented in *Entertainment Weekly,* "I didn't know whom to relate to as I read *Blubber;* I wanted to believe that I wasn't like Jill, but at the same time, Linda was infuriatingly weak. The book, unlike others written for girls my age, refused to tell me how to feel. And yet, looking back, it's rich with revealing symbolism."

In 1977, Blume published what she describes as her most autobiographical novel. *Starring Sally J. Freedman as Herself* is the story of a 10-year-old girl named Sally who moves with her family from New Jersey to Miami Beach in 1947. American adults are returning to their normal lives after the end of World War II, but Sally has lingering fears about the war. She is convinced that Mr. Zavodsky, a man who lives in her apartment building, is actually Adolph Hitler disguised and in hiding. Sally knows that Hitler wanted to kill all Jewish people, and since she is Jewish, she believes Mr. Zavodsky is trying to poison her. She wonders what to do about Mr. Zavodsky, but at the same time, her year in Miami Beach also includes new friends and experiences, her first crush on a boy, and many other adventures.

"Sally J. Freedman is my most autobiographical character," Blume revealed. "She is the kind of child I was at nine and ten, when I was the most interesting." That connection was noted by the reviewer for *School Library Journal*. "Clearly there is much of Judy Blume in the main character and her affection for Sally shines through. The novel is as pertinent today as it was when first published."

"Judy Blume excels at describing how it feels to be invisible," Diablo Cody wrote in **Entertainment Weekly.** *"Every other book written for kids my age was sunny, upbeat, and about as subtle as a bullhorn-wielding camp counselor. Blume's stuff had an edge; it was grimly hilarious and worthy of my attention."*

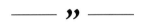

Blume published *Just as Long as We're Together* in 1987. In this book, she tells the story of Rachel and Stephanie, best friends who share everything. Then in seventh grade, Alison moves into the neighborhood. Stephanie wants to include Alison in things that she used to share only with Rachel, and that's when things start to get complicated. *Washington Post Book World* reviewer Beryl Lieff Benderly observed, "While apparently presenting the bright, slangy, surface details of life in an upper-middle class suburban junior high school, she's really plumbing the meaning of honesty, friendship, loyalty, secrecy, individuality, and the painful, puzzling question of what we owe those we love."

In 1993, Blume published *Here's to You, Rachel Robinson* as a companion book to *Just as Long as We're Together*. This book revisits the characters in-

Blume has acknowledged that Sally J. Freedman is her most autobiographical character, based on herself as a child.

troduced in *Just as Long as We're Together*, picking up the story at the end of seventh grade. Perfectionist Rachel is stressed out about school and problems at home. Her older brother Charles has been kicked out of boarding school and is causing all kinds of trouble. Everyone keeps telling Rachel to "lighten up" but that isn't so easy to do. *Here's to You, Rachel Robinson* and *Just as Long as We're Together* continue to appeal to readers, and in 2007 they were republished as a two-book edition titled *BFF**.

As a reviewer noted in *Publisher's Weekly*, "Rachel's incisive, first-person narration easily draws readers into her complicated world as she learns to cope with the pressures brought on by her relentless quest to be the best at everything and by her troubled family situation. Perceptive, strong storytelling ensures that other characters' points of view (particularly Rachel's brother's) can also be discerned. Blume once again demonstrates her ability to shape multidimensional characters and to explore—often through very convincing dialogue—the tangled interactions of believable, complex people."

Books for Younger Readers

Along with her many novels for teens and pre-teens, Blume has also published books for younger readers. Some of her most beloved books are those about Fudge, with stories derived from her own family. According to Blume, "Fudge is based on my son, Larry, when he was a toddler." *Tales of a Fourth Grade Nothing* (1972) is the first of a five-book series about Peter and his little brother Fudge. Everyone else seems to think Fudge is so cute, but to Peter, Fudge is nothing but an annoying little troublemaker. That resonated with *Entertainment Weekly* contributor Diablo Cody, who wrote this about *Tales of a Fourth-Grade Nothing*: "Judy Blume excels at describing how it feels to be invisible.… Every other book written for kids my age was sunny, upbeat, and about as subtle as a bullhorn-wielding camp counselor. Blume's stuff had an edge; it was grimly hilarious and worthy of my attention."

Blume followed that with the second book in the Fudge series, *Otherwise Known As Sheila the Great* (1972). This installment focuses on Peter's nemesis Sheila Tubman as she grapples with the challenges of scary dogs and the dreaded swimming lessons. In *Superfudge* (1980), Peter learns that a new baby will soon join the family. Now Peter will have to deal with many big changes at home in addition to putting up with Fudge. A *New York Times Book Review* called *Superfudge* "a genuinely funny story … dealing with the kinks and knots of modern family life." Things only get worse for Peter as the story continues with *Fudge-a-Mania* (1990). In this book, Peter learns that his family is going on summer vacation to a cottage right next door to Sheila Tubman's family. *Publishers Weekly* praised *Fudge-a-Mania* as a "fast-pitched, funny novel.… The colorful antics of all members of the two families makes reading these pages a treat." Blume wrote *Double Fudge* (2002), the final book in the Fudge series, at the request of her grandson. Now in seventh grade, Peter must cope with the usual annoyances plus the antics of his eccentric cousins.

In 1984, Blume published *The Pain and the Great One*, a picture book for very young readers. She later developed a new series based on that picture book—chapter books for readers aged five to eight that featured the same characters as those in *The Pain and the Great One.* The books in this series include short stories about the adventures of eight-year-old Abigail and her six-year-old brother Jake. *Soupy Saturdays* was published in 2007, followed by *Cool Zone* and *Going, Going, Gone* in 2008, and *Friend or Fiend?*, the last Pain and the Great One book, in 2009. A *Booklist* review noted, "Blume's singular ability to portray the minutiae of a child's everyday life with humor is perfectly complemented by … occasional line drawings that extend the story's charm and fully shaped characters." *Kirkus Reviews* observed, "Once again, Blume shows off her pitch-perfect understanding of childhood anxieties and family dynamics."

Books for Teens

Like her books for middle-grade readers, Blume's novels for teens have remained popular with generations of readers. In *Forever* and *Tiger Eyes*, she explored the coming-of-age stories of teen characters who must navigate through difficult emotional situations. These books focus on mature themes such as teenage sexuality, death, and the grief process. Blume's direct, honest writing about teens struggling with critical life experiences added to her reputation for taking on taboo subjects.

Blume published *Forever,* her ground-breaking and perhaps most controversial book, in 1975. *Forever* is the story of Katherine, a high school senior who falls in love for the first time. Katherine meets Michael at a New Year's Eve party and the two quickly become devoted to each other. As their relationship develops, they make a conscious decision to have sex. When they finally do, they both pledge to love each other "forever." But as time passes and the two are separated for the summer, Katherine begins to see things differently.

Forever caused a stir when it was first published, primarily due to Blume's frank and direct writing about sex between two teenagers. Blume did not

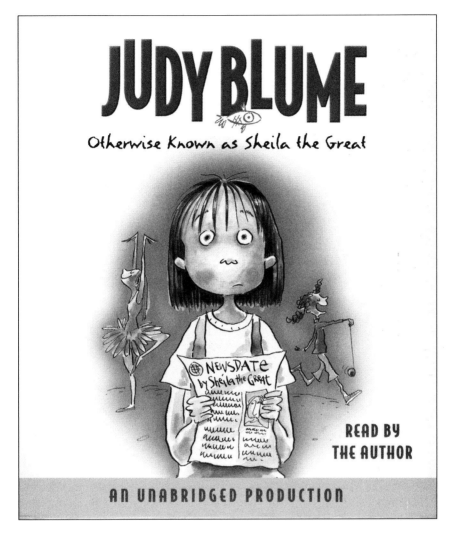

The Fudge *books have been popular for decades, with generations of new readers enjoying them in print, as audio books, and as e-books.*

set out to write a controversial book, and was somewhat surprised by the response *Forever* received from some adults. "My 14-year-old daughter was reading a lot of books that equated sex with punishment. She said, 'Couldn't there ever be a book about two nice, smart kids who do it, and nobody has to die?' I thought, yeah, we're not doing anybody any favor by all of this sex linked with punishment. That's really why I wrote it," Blume explained. "I wanted to present another kind of story—one in which two seniors in high school fall in love, decide together to have sex, and act responsibly."

23

———— " ————

"I believe that censorship grows out of fear, and because fear is contagious, some parents are easily swayed," Blume argued. "Book banning satisfies their need to feel in control of their children's lives…. They want to believe that if their children don't read about it, their children won't know about it. And if they don't know about it, it won't happen."

———— " ————

Some adults saw *Forever* as a realistic portrayal of teen romance, what the *New York Times Book Review* called "a convincing account of first love." Others protested that the book was too explicit and that it sent the wrong message to teens. They argued that the book made it acceptable for teens to be sexually active, Fueled by these objections, *Forever* became one of the most banned books in America. Since 1990, *Forever* has consistently been ranked among the top 10 on the American Library Association's list of the 100 Most Challenged Books.

That controversy continues today, as seen in this recent remark by NPR commentator J. Courtney Sullivan. "What shocks me is that in the age of sexting, Bristol Palin, and online porn, *Forever* is still considered controversial. At its core, it's about female teenagers who make responsible birth control choices—who, when they're ready, have sex on their own terms, instead of for the gaze or approval of men. What's so shocking about that?" *Seattle Post-Intelligencer* book reviewer Cecelia Goodnow noted, "*Forever*, a teen novel that was deemed racy in the 1970s, is undeniably frank about a teenage girl's sexual initiation. But there's also something wistfully innocent, from today's vantage point, in a girl who dates and falls in love instead of 'hooking up.' Katherine even introduces her boyfriend Michael to her parents. What a concept, and one that's bound to give contemporary parents a pang for the good old days."

In 1981, Blume published *Tiger Eyes,* another book for teens. *Tiger Eyes* is the story of Davey, a young girl whose father is tragically killed in a robbery. Soon after, Davey goes with her mother and younger brother to visit relatives in New Mexico. Struggling with grief over her father's death, Davey becomes friends with a young man who helps her find the strength to begin to heal. "Although there's a violent crime at the center of the story, *Tiger Eyes* isn't about violence," Blume explained. "It's about the sudden, tragic loss of someone you love. I lost my beloved father suddenly, when I was 21. He died, not as the result of a violent crime, but of a heart attack at

#1 *NEW YORK TIMES* BESTSELLING AUTHOR

judy blume

forever...

Is there a difference between first love and true love?

Forever, *a portrayal of teen romance, is Blume's most controversial work and a frequent target of censorship. The novel is one of five of her books on the American Library Association's list of the 100 most challenged books.*

home. I was with him. I still can't write this without choking up, remembering. Davey's feelings about her father's sudden death were based on mine, though I'm not sure I was aware of it while I was writing the book.

"I lived in Los Alamos, New Mexico, the setting of the book, for two years. My teenaged children went to school there. It wasn't a happy experience.… It allowed me to write about a world I would never have known, about characters I'd never have imagined. Yet I didn't start to write this book until I'd left the town (and the relationship that took me there) and was able to look back. Someday, I hope, Larry will direct the film version." Indeed, Blume worked with her son Lawrence to produce a feature film based on *Tiger Eyes*. The movie premiered at the 2012 International Film Festival in Sonoma, California. *Filmmaker Magazine* movie critic Lauren Wissot praised *Tiger Eyes* as "the rarest of family films, smart and nuanced, with an attention to detail in images that mirrors what is Ms. Blume's strength with words."

Responding to Censorship

During the 1980s, several of Blume's books became the target of organized book-banning campaigns in schools and public libraries across the country. Some adults objected to her use of profanity in her books, the mature themes of some stories, and the straightforward discussions of sexuality. Others found fault with the books' ambiguous or unresolved endings, which left readers to form their own conclusions. Unlike most previously published novels for younger readers, Blume's books did not provide simple or clear solutions to characters' problems. For these reasons, some parents felt that her books were inappropriate and even harmful for young people to read.

Blume disagreed strongly with those who felt her books were wrong for kids. "I believe that censorship grows out of fear, and because fear is contagious, some parents are easily swayed," she argued. "Book banning satisfies their need to feel in control of their children's lives. This fear is often disguised as moral outrage. They want to believe that if their children don't read about it, their children won't know about it. And if they don't know about it, it won't happen."

"I wrote these books a long time ago when there wasn't anything near the censorship that there is now. I wasn't aware at the time that I was writing anything controversial. I just know what these books would have meant to me when I was a kid," Blume explained. "I knew intuitively what kids wanted to know because I remembered what I wanted to know. I think I write about sexuality because it was uppermost in my mind when I was a kid: the need to know, and not knowing how to find out."

Blume is shown here in her tap dance class, one of her many hobbies.

Blume has been a fixture on the American Library Association's list of the most-challenged authors since the early 1980s. From 1982 to 1996, Blume was ranked the number one Most Challenged Author. Five of her books are on the American Library Association's list of the 100 Most Challenged Books (*Forever, Blubber, Deenie, Tiger Eyes,* and *Are You There God? It's Me, Margaret*). The campaigns against her books inspired Blume to work with the National Coalition against Censorship to protect the freedom to read.

In 1996, Blume won the Margaret A. Edwards Award for *Forever* from the Young Adult Library Services Association (YALSA), a division of the American Library Association. For Blume, whose books have won a lot of awards, this one was particularly gratifying. "Winning an award is always an honor but it doesn't always affect your personal or professional life. Winning the Margaret A. Edwards Award has made a profound difference for me, both personally and professionally. By honoring a controversial book like *Forever* YALSA has sent a message—We're not afraid of challenges. We're prepared to defend books that teens want to read. It gives me heft when I speak out in defense of someone else's book. It reminds me that I'm far from alone in the fight for intellectual freedom.… I'm deeply grateful to YALSA for recognizing my work. To have an award that's described as 'honoring writers whose work has helped YA readers understand themselves and their world ...' well, it's enough to make you want to sit down and start another novel."

> "*I wasn't aware at the time that I was writing anything controversial. I just know what these books would have meant to me when I was a kid," Blume explained. "I knew intuitively what kids wanted to know because I remembered what I wanted to know. I think I write about sexuality because it was uppermost in my mind when I was a kid: the need to know, and not knowing how to find out.*

Some of Blume's books continue to be challenged or restricted in schools and public libraries, but her popularity with readers and critics has remained strong. That's because her work reflects real life, according to Natalie Babbitt, author of the children's classics *Tuck Everlasting* and *The Eyes of the Amaryllis.* "Some parents and librarians have come down hard on Judy Blume for the occasional vulgarities in her stories," Babbitt wrote in the *New York Times Book Review.* "Blume's vulgarities, however, exist in real life and are presented in her books with honesty and full acceptance." Blume has received a host of awards over her long career, including several recent prestigious awards. In 2000, she was honored by the Library of Congress with a Living Legends Award. In 2004, she received the National Book Foundation award for distinguished contributions to American letters. This was the first time that this prestigious award was given to an author of books for children and young adults. In 2011, Blume was recognized by the Smithsonian Associates with the John P. McGovern Award for contributions to the American family.

Blume and her work have been greeted with controversy and book banning as well as popular and critical acclaim. But controversy hasn't changed Blume—and neither have honors and awards. "I don't think people change,"she explained.'Everything around us changes, but the human condition doesn't change. What's important to us remains the same, and that's what links everyone together. It's that inside stuff: the need for love and acceptance, and getting to know yourself and your place in the world."

MARRIAGE AND FAMILY

In 1959, Blume married her first husband, John Blume. They had two children, a daughter named Randy Lee, born in 1961, and a son named Lawrence Andrew, born in 1963. The couple divorced in 1975. In 1976, Blume married Thomas Kitchens, and the marriage ended in divorce in 1979. In 1987, Blume married George Cooper, with whom she has a step-daughter named Amanda.

Blume currently lives with her husband George. They spend most of the year in Key West, Florida, and also own homes in New York City and Martha's Vineyard, an island off the coast of Massachusetts.

HOBBIES AND OTHER INTERESTS

Blume founded then non-profit KIDS Fund in 1981. KIDS Fund is an organization that contributes thousands of dollars each year to programs that help children talk with their parents. In her spare time, Blume enjoys going to the movies, seeing plays, reading, dancing, kayaking, bicycling, needlepoint, and baseball. She is a fan of the New York Mets.

SELECTED WRITINGS

For Young Readers

The One in the Middle Is the Green Kangaroo, 1969
Freckle Juice, 1971
Tales of a Fourth Grade Nothing, 1972
Otherwise Known as Sheila the Great, 1972
Superfudge, 1980
The Pain and the Great One, 1984
Fudge-a-Mania, 1990
Double Fudge, 2002

Soupy Saturdays with the Pain and the Great One, 2007
Cool Zone with the Pain and the Great One, 2008
Going, Going, Gone! With the Pain and the Great One, 2008
Friend or Fiend? With the Pain and the Great One, 2009

For Middle-Grade Readers

Iggie's House, 1970
Are You There God? It's Me, Margaret, 1970
Then Again, Maybe I Won't, 1971
It's Not the End of the World, 1972
Deenie, 1973
Blubber, 1974
Starring Sally J. Freedman as Herself, 1977
Just as Long as We're Together, 1987
Here's to You, Rachel Robinson, 1993
BFF*, 2007 (includes *Just as Long as We're Together* and *Here's to You, Rachel Robinson*)

For Teens

Forever, 1975
Tiger Eyes, 1981

For Adults

Wifey, 1978
Smart Women, 1983
Summer Sisters, 1998

HONORS AND AWARDS

Outstanding Book of the Year (*New York Times*): 1970, for *Are You There God? It's Me, Margaret*; 1974, for *Blubber*
Eleanor Roosevelt Humanitarian Awards: 1983
Children's Choice Awards (International Reading Association and Children's Book Council): 1981, for *Superfudge*; 1985, for *The Pain and the Great One*
Best Books for Young Adults (*School Library Journal*): 1981, for *Tiger Eyes*
Books for the Teen Age (New York Public Library): 1982, for *Tiger Eyes*
Dorothy Canfield Fisher Children's Book Award: 1983, for *Tiger Eyes*
National Hero Awards (Big Brothers/Big Sisters): 1992
Parents' Choice Awards (Parents' Choice Foundation): 1993, for *Here's to You, Rachel Robinson*
Margaret A. Edwards Awards for Outstanding Literature for Young Adults (YALSA-American Library Association): 1996, for *Forever*
Living Legends Award (Library of Congress): 2000

Medal for Distinguished Contribution to American Letters (National Book Foundation): 2004

All-Time 100 Novels List (Time magazine): 2005, for *Are You There God? It's Me, Margaret*

John P. McGovern Award (Smithsonian Associates): 2011, for contributions to the American family

FURTHER READING

Periodicals

Cosmo Girl, June 2002

Entertainment Weekly, Oct. 3, 2008, p.32

Instructor, May/June 2005, pg.37

New York Times, Nov. 16, 1997; Nov. 14, 2004, p.L1

Newsweek, June 1990

School Library Journal, June 1996, p.24

Seattle Post-Intelligencer, Sep. 13, 2007

Seventeen, Oct. 2007

Smithsonian, Jan. 2012

Online Articles

bookclubs.barnesandnoble.com/t5/The-NOOK-Blog/Guest-Author-Judy-Blume/ba-p/1225280
    (Barnes and Noble, "Guest Author: Judy Blume,"Dec. 7, 2011)

www.januarymagazine.com/profiles/blume.html
    (January Magazine, "Judy Blume,"no date)

www.kindlepost.com/2012/01/guest-blogger-judy-blume-.html
    (Kindle Daily Post, "Guest Blogger: Judy Blume,"Jan. 27, 2012)

www.npr.org/2011/11/28/142859819/judy-blume-banned-often-but-widely-beloved
    (NPR, "Judy Blume: Often Banned, But Widely Beloved,"Nov. 28, 2011)

www.randomhouse.com/boldtype/0698/blume/interview.html
    (Random House, "Alison Dorfman Interviews Judy Blume,"no date)

www.scholastic.com/teachers/article/judy-blume-interview-transcript
    (Scholastic, "Judy Blume Interview Transcript,"no date)

ADDRESS

Judy Blume
Children's Publicity
1745 Broadway
New York, NY 10019

WEB SITE

www.judyblume.com

Ellen DeGeneres 1958-

American Actor, Comedian, and Talk Show Host
Award-Winning Host of the Hit TV Talk Show "The
Ellen DeGeneres Show"

BIRTH

Ellen DeGeneres was born on January 26, 1958, in Metarie,
Louisiana. Her father, Elliot, sold insurance. Her mother, Betty,
worked as a secretary. She has one older brother, named Vance.

YOUTH

As a child, DeGeneres was shy and quiet. She loved animals
and thought of becoming a veterinarian. But she gave up on

this idea when she realized that she wasn't "book smart" enough for veterinarian school. She liked to spend time alone, writing and dreaming of becoming a singer. "I wanted to be a singer and a songwriter. I love music and singing, and like a lot of young girls who are lonely, I sat at home and wrote songs and poetry, and that's something I could do. And then it turned out I was better at being funny."

When DeGeneres was growing up her family moved around a lot, and they lived in different places in and around the city of New Orleans. "We never owned a house when I was growing up," she recalled. "We rented, and we moved about every two years, just far enough to have to start at a new school." Her parents divorced when she was 13 years old. After the divorce, DeGeneres and her brother moved with their mother to the small town of Atlanta, Texas.

> *"I wanted to be a singer and a songwriter," DeGeneres said about her childhood plans. "I love music and singing, and like a lot of young girls who are lonely, I sat at home and wrote songs and poetry, and that's something I could do. And then it turned out I was better at being funny."*

DeGeneres's mother married again, but the relationship lasted only a few years. When Ellen was 16 years old, she was molested by her stepfather. She did not tell anyone about the abuse right away, because her mother was undergoing treatment for breast cancer at the time. Many years later she explained that decision. "I really didn't want to have to talk about it, but at the same time, the statistics are that one in three women have been molested in some way, and that's a pretty high statistic. And there should be more people talking about it; it shouldn't be a shameful thing. It is never your fault. So I don't mind talking about it. He did horrible things to me and he was a bad man. I should have told Mother right away.... You should always, always tell somebody."

EDUCATION

DeGeneres attended public elementary schools in New Orleans and went to high school in Atlanta, Texas. After graduating from high school in 1976, she moved back to New Orleans. She enrolled in the University of New Orleans but only attended classes for half of one semester. "I hated school. I started college because everyone else was going. I majored in communications, I think. Or communications and drama. And I just remember sit-

DeGeneres performing stand up at The Improv comedy club in the 1980s.

ting in there, and they were talking about the history of Greek theater or something, and thinking,'This is not what I want to know.'"

CAREER HIGHLIGHTS

After dropping out of college, DeGeneres supported herself by working at a variety of different jobs. She worked as a waitress, a bartender, and a house painter. At one point, she had a job shucking oysters. She sold clothing and vacuum cleaners, and was a legal secretary for a short time. DeGeneres was good at some of these jobs, but she always ran into problems following rules. "I realized I needed to find something where I didn't have to answer to a boss. I slowly started to discover what I wanted."

DeGeneres had always had a talent for making people laugh. When she was 23 years old, she began performing stand-up comedy at the open mic night at a local coffee house. From there, she went on to perform stand-up comedy gigs at area colleges and universities. Her stand-up comedy routines were based on her funny observations of normal, everyday life. "I watch people's behavior and I notice things. I think that's why I became a comedian. I notice how stupid the things we do are."

Becoming a Comedian and an Actor

In 1981, DeGeneres landed a job as the emcee at Clyde's Comedy Club in the New Orleans entertainment district known as the French Quarter. At that time, Clyde's was the only comedy club in the city. As the club's emcee, DeGeneres performed stand-up comedy routines and introduced the other comedians who appeared at the club.

DeGeneres moved to Los Angeles, California, after Clyde's Comedy Club closed. She performed in stand-up comedy clubs around Los Angeles, re-fining her jokes and developing new comedy routines. One of her most well-known comedy bits from this time period was titled "Phone Call to God." In this monologue, DeGeneres pretends to call God to ask about things that had always bothered her, such as why God created fleas. "Phone Call to God" quickly became her most popular comedy routine and soon led to bigger opportunities.

DeGeneres began performing at the Los Angeles comedy club The Improv, a famous comedy club (now a chain of clubs) where many comedians got their start. "I had a friend in L.A. who knew the owner of the Improv," she recalled. "We went to see him, I auditioned, and he gave me some great spots. Instead of having to wait around for hours like the rest of the begin-ning comics, he had me booked into good time slots." In 1982, DeGeneres was named the Funniest Person in America by the cable television channel Showtime. She went on to become the opening act for Jay Leno. This was earlier in Leno's career, when he was one of America's top stand-up come-dians and was not yet a late-night TV host.

DeGeneres made her TV debut in 1986 on "The Tonight Show Starring Johnny Carson." This was a different era in TV, a time when there were very few TV networks and very few choices about what to watch. As the king of late-night TV, Carson was one of the most influential people in the entertainment industry. DeGeneres's first stand-up comedy performance on "The Tonight Show" was a huge success. She was surprised and thrilled when Carson invited her over to sit on the couch and chat after she fin-ished her monologue. That was an honor usually reserved for the very best comedians; in fact, DeGeneres was the first female comedian he had ever invited over. Carson's endorsement led to appearances on several comedy specials produced by the HBO cable TV network. Throughout the late 1980s, DeGeneres made regular appearances on HBO.

DeGeneres made the transition from stand-up comedian to actor in 1989. She had small roles in several different situation comedies, beginning with "Open House" on the Fox network. In 1991, she won the American Come-dy Award for Best Female Comedy Club Stand-Up Performer. She had a recurring role in the 1992 ABC series "Laurie Hill" and appeared in the 1993 movie *Coneheads*.

A cast shot from the TV series "Laurie Hill," an early acting job.
DeGeneres is second from the right.

"Ellen"

In 1994, DeGeneres landed her first major acting role as part of the ensemble cast of the ABC situation comedy "These Friends of Mine." DeGeneres played Ellen Morgan, a clerk in a bookstore coffeehouse who was always preoccupied with making a good impression on everyone around her. Over the course of the first season, her character grew into a leading role. After the first season, the network renamed the show "Ellen" and made DeGeneres the star.

Beginning in the second season of "Ellen," the focus shifted to highlight DeGeneres's humor and comedic delivery. She patterned her performances on Lucille Ball in "I Love Lucy," a popular TV comedy series that aired in the late 1950s. "I knew what I could do with it," she remarked. "I wanted to do a smarter, hipper version of 'I Love Lucy.' I wanted a show that everybody talks about the next day."

Episodes of "Ellen" were based on Ellen Morgan's adventures and mishaps at work, in relationships, and funny situations and circumstances. DeGeneres described Ellen Morgan as "this person who's desperate to make everyone happy. Unfortunately, when she does that, she ends up putting her foot in her mouth."

"Ellen" became an instant hit show that attracted record-breaking ratings week after week. As the popularity of "Ellen" grew, DeGeneres became more recognizable and more well-known. She had mixed feelings about her rise to fame. In a 1994 interview in *TV Guide*, DeGeneres said, "If the show is successful, then you're reaching millions of people. But you're also standing there naked, saying, 'What do you think of me?' And there are mean people who just want to tear you apart. That kind of frightens me.… I try not to, but I worry about everything."

For her work on "Ellen," DeGeneres received multiple Golden Globe and Screen Actors Guild nominations, and was nominated for the Emmy Award for Best Actress for every season of the show. In 1995, while continuing work on "Ellen," DeGeneres published her first book, *My Point … And I Do Have One*. This collection of some of her better-known comedy sketches debuted at number one on the *New York Times* Bestseller list.

In 1996, DeGeneres landed her first starring role in a movie. In the dark romantic comedy *Mr. Wrong*, she played Martha, a woman who falls in love with a handsome stranger, played by Bill Pullman. But Martha's life is turned upside down as she soon discovers that her dream man is not as perfect as she thought he was. *Mr. Wrong* was panned by critics and was only moderately successful with moviegoers.

A Turning Point

During the fourth season of "Ellen," DeGeneres made an important personal and professional decision. She decided that it was time for both herself and her character Ellen Morgan to come out as lesbian. This was a risky decision because the only gay characters seen on TV were in supporting roles. At that time, homosexuality was not widely accepted. Most gay and lesbian entertainers were in the closet, or secretive, about their sexual orientation. Very few entertainers were open about being gay, and there were no leading characters that were gay. In spite of the risk involved, DeGeneres felt that it was something she needed to do.

"I mean, you get used to living with secrets, because I did," DeGeneres explained. "There are people out there hiding all kinds of things. People who have all this success and all this fame and all this money, and yet there are secrets that they think if we found out about, it would be over for them. And it's a horrible way to live whether you're famous or not. You could just be somebody at home with a bunch of kids, and hiding something from the ladies at the PTA. That's a horrible way to live."

DeGeneres worked with the writers of "Ellen" to create the episode in which her character would reveal that she was gay. Titled "The Puppy

Allen County Public Library
Thursday October 30 2014 04:12AM

Barcode: 31833046239213
Title: Going to the doctor
Type: BOOK
Due date: 11/20/2014,23:59

Barcode: 31833067555760
Title: The incomplete book of dragons :.
..
Type: BOOK
Due date: 11/20/2014,23:59

Barcode: 31833063939554
Title: Biography today : profiles of pe.
..
Type: MAGAZINE
Due date: 11/20/2014,23:59

Total items checked out: 3

Telephone Renewal: (219)421-1240
Website Renewal: www.acpl.info

A scene from "The Puppy Episode": DeGeneres with Laura Dern at the airport, standing at the microphone.

Episode," it features a mix of serious themes and humor. The story revolves around Ellen Morgan's growing realization that she is attracted to Susan, a woman she recently met (played by Laura Dern). Ellen struggles with this new awareness and talks to a therapist (played by Oprah Winfrey). Thinking that Susan is leaving town, Ellen follows her to the airport. When she tries to talk to Susan, Ellen accidentally announces that she is gay over a loudspeaker in the crowded airport. She is then afraid to tell her friends, but eventually does with the help of one of her neighbors.

"The Puppy Episode" aired in 1997 and was the highest-rated episode of "Ellen," drawing a record 46 million viewers. DeGeneres won the prestigious Peabody Award and an Emmy Award for the critically acclaimed episode. She was named the Entertainer of the Year for 1997 and 1998 by *Entertainment Weekly* magazine and received the 1998 GLAAD Stephen F. Kolzak Award.

Controversy and Consequences

But "The Puppy Episode" was also very controversial. DeGeneres's public confirmation that she was gay in real life became national headline news. She came under attack from political and religious conservative groups who accused her of promoting homosexuality. She was also criticized by some in the gay community. "There were extreme groups that didn't think I was gay enough. There were other groups of people who thought I was too gay. It didn't occur to me that when I announced I was gay I would have to clarify just how gay I was," DeGeneres said. "I never wanted to be the lesbian actress. I never wanted to be the spokesperson for the gay community. Ever. I did it for my own truth."

The controversy over DeGeneres's decision to come out on national TV proved to be too much for the network. "Ellen" was cancelled in 1998. De-Generes was out of a job, and she also found herself suddenly and unexpectedly without any prospects for work. In spite of her past success, no one would hire her. The backlash also affected actor Laura Dern, who played Ellen's love interest in "The Puppy Episode." Dern was unable to find work as an actor for almost a year after the episode aired.

"Even though I had a big foundation with my career and years of work, it just divided everyone when I came out," DeGeneres revealed. "Simply my saying I was gay—even though I was the exact same person—divided everyone. People stopped watching the show, so some advertisers pulled out. It didn't matter that I was a good, devoted, loyal employee. I mean, I showed up on time. I never did anything wrong. I was kind. I was easy to work with. And yet it was the dollar that mattered more. It was just a huge dose of reality for me. But losing it all really gave me time to realize that all this stuff is very fleeting. If success is really dependent on someone liking you or not liking you, and you have to teeter on that kind of tightrope of how you're supposed to act and how you're supposed to look and who you are, it's just not a healthy way to live. Now I get to be me every single day and not have to worry about hiding anything at all."

By 1999, DeGeneres was starting to rebuild her career. That year, she appeared in two movies, *The Love Letter*, a romantic comedy about mistaken identity, and *EDtv*, a comedy about a reality show taken to the extreme. In 2000, she was featured in the HBO production *If These Walls Could Talk II*, a set of three separate stories of lesbian couples in different time periods. She also appeared as a guest on "The Larry Sanders Show," a role for which she received an Emmy nomination.

In 2001, DeGeneres created and starred in the CBS situation comedy "The Ellen Show." She played Ellen Richmond, an entrepreneur who returns to her small hometown after her company fails. She gets a job as a counselor at the local high school and learns to adjust to the slower pace of life in the small community. Though "The Ellen Show" was critically acclaimed, ratings were low and only 18 episodes were produced. "The Ellen Show" was cancelled in its first season.

*DeGeneres dancing with First Lady Michelle Obama on
"The Ellen DeGeneres Show."*

"The Ellen DeGeneres Show"

DeGeneres found success once again with "The Ellen DeGeneres Show," a daily TV talk show that began airing in 2003. "The Ellen DeGeneres Show" is described on its web site as "the daytime destination for laughter and fun." Each episode of the show begins with DeGeneres talking for a few minutes about whatever is on her mind that day, often including her personal observations on current events or topics of everyday life. This segment of the show is always followed by DeGeneres dancing through the studio—she is known for her love of dancing—with the whole audience dancing along with her.

Episodes of "The Ellen DeGeneres Show" typically feature a mix of entertainment and interviews with popular celebrities, musicians, politicians, and other notable people. Her interviews include a playful quality that seems to put people at ease and encourages her guests to relax and chat. She sometimes appears star-struck, as awed by her famous guests as her audience would be. "The Ellen DeGeneres Show" often showcases performances by both established stars and unknown musicians. DeGeneres has gained a reputation for finding talented performers on the Internet and inviting these new artists to appear on her show. Other popular features are the frequent audience participation contests, games, and prize give-aways. She has also created special segments of the show that highlight funny photos and text messages sent in by viewers.

> *"I think we need more love in the world. We need more kindness, more compassion, more joy, more laughter,"* DeGeneres stressed. *"The most important thing for me is to know that I represent kindness. I'm glad I'm funny. I'm glad I make people happy, because that's very important. But I'm proud to be known as a kind person."*

"The Ellen DeGeneres Show" quickly became a hit with daytime viewers as well as TV critics. "Ellen just gets people—whether they're celebrities or plain folks," wrote *Redbook* TV critic John Griffits. "It's no wonder that millions of people tune into 'The Ellen DeGeneres Show' each day, or that Hollywood's biggest stars are jumping at the chance to be her guests. She says what we're thinking. She zeroes in on all the weird and wonderful things that make life great—like bells on bicycles, singing parrots, and good, old-fashioned sneakers." Since its debut in 2003, "The Ellen DeGeneres Show" has earned numerous Daytime Emmy Awards and People's Choice Awards, a Teen Choice Award, a Genesis Award, and a GLAAD Media Award.

The popularity of "The Ellen DeGeneres Show" propelled DeGeneres back to the top of the entertainment industry. She has been named among the *Forbes* 100 Most Powerful Women, *Time* magazine's 100 Most Influential People, and *Entertainment Weekly*'s 50 Most Powerful Entertainers. She has hosted the Primetime Emmy Awards broadcast three times, the Grammy Awards show twice, and the Academy Awards TV broadcast.

A Versatile Entertainer

DeGeneres is a versatile entertainer who has stayed active in many enter-tainment arenas in addition to her TV talk show. She returned to movie acting as the voice of Dory, a fish who has trouble remembering things, in the 2003 animated feature *Finding Nemo.* She also published her second book *The Funny Thing Is ...* that year. This collection of short stories and essays was an immediate best-seller. DeGeneres was nominated for a 2005 Grammy Award for Best Comedy Album for her reading of the

DeGeneres voiced the character of Dory in Finding Nemo.

audio version of the book. In 2010, she was a judge on the popular TV singing competition show "American Idol" for one season. Also in 2010, she founded the eleveneleven record label with the goal of discovering new musical talent. DeGeneres published her third book *Seriously ... I'm Kidding* in 2011. This collection of photos, quotes, and stories from her life includes her thoughts on meditation, gambling, pets, the importance of being on time, and more.

Throughout the ups and downs of her long career, DeGeneres has managed to maintain perspective. "I'm definitely happier than I've ever been. I assume tomorrow I'll be happier than today, because things are great. I have a great career and I have wonderful fans who really are supportive and loyal—because I'm not hiding anything from them. So, on the spectrum of happiness, I'm pretty high up there."

"I believe everything in life is energy. If we're destroying our trees and destroying our environment and hurting animals and hurting one another and all that stuff, there's got to be a very powerful energy to fight that. I think we need more love in the world. We need more kindness, more compassion, more joy, more laughter. I definitely want my time here to be positive and productive," DeGeneres stressed. "The most important thing for me is to know that I represent kindness. I'm glad I'm funny. I'm glad I make people happy, because that's very important. But I'm proud to be known as a kind person."

MARRIAGE AND FAMILY

DeGeneres married actor Portia de Rossi in 2008. They live in Beverly Hills, California.

HOBBIES AND OTHER INTERESTS

DeGeneres is active in many humanitarian causes, particularly campaigns against bullying. She works closely with The Trevor Project and the Pacer Center to educate and raise awareness about bullying. She founded the United Against Bullying campaign to promote the message "be kind to one another." DeGeneres also promotes animal welfare through her work with animal rescue organizations such as Gentle Barn.

In her spare time, DeGeneres enjoys gardening, hunting for antiques, and interior design. "Designing is my hobby. If I didn't do what I do for a living—at some point when I don't do this for a living—I'll probably just do design work.... I enjoy putting rooms together." She collects old paintings and photographs of people, and enjoys spending time with her many pets.

SELECTED CREDITS

Books

My Point ... And I Do Have One, 1995
The Funny Thing Is ..., 2003
Seriously ... I'm Kidding, 2011

Movies

Mr. Wrong, 1996
EDtv, 1999
The Love Letter, 1999
Finding Nemo, 2003

Television

"Ellen," 1994-1998 (series)
If These Walls Could Talk II, 2000 (special)
"The Ellen Show," 2001-2002 (series)
"The Ellen DeGeneres Show," 2003- (talk show)

HONORS AND AWARDS

Funniest Person in America (Showtime): 1982
American Comedy Awards: 1991, Best Female Comedy Club Stand-Up
  Performer

Golden Apple Awards (Hollywood Women's Press Association): 1994, Female Discovery of the Year

Entertainer of the Year (*Entertainment Weekly*): 1997 and 1998

Peabody Awards: 1998, for writing of "The Puppy Episode" of "Ellen"

Stephen F. Kolzak Awards (GLAAD): 1998

Annie Awards (International Animated Film Association): 2004, Outstanding Voice Acting, for *Finding Nemo*

Daytime Emmy Awards (National Academy of Television Arts and Sciences): 2004, Outstanding Talk Show; 2005 (3 awards), Outstanding Talk Show, Outstanding Talk Show Host, and Outstanding Special Class Writing; 2006 (3 awards), Outstanding Talk Show, Outstanding Talk Show Host, and Outstanding Special Class Writing; 2007 (3 awards), Outstanding Talk Show, Outstanding Talk Show Host, and Outstanding Special Class Writing; 2008 (2 awards), Outstanding Talk Show and Outstanding Talk Show Host; 2010, Outstanding Talk Show; 2011, Outstanding Talk Show

Kids Choice Awards (Nickelodeon): 2004, Favorite Voice from an Animated Movie, for *Finding Nemo*

Saturn Awards (Academy of Science Fiction, Fantasy & Horror): 2004, Best Supporting Actress, for *Finding Nemo*

People's Choice Awards: 2005 (2 awards), Favorite Funny Female Star and Favorite Talk Show Host; 2006 (2 awards), Favorite Funny Female Star and Favorite Talk Show Host; 2007 (2 awards), Favorite Funny Female Star and Favorite Talk Show Host; 2008 (2 awards), Favorite Funny Female Star and Favorite Talk Show Host; 2009, Favorite Talk Show Host; 2010 (2 awards), Favorite Talk Show Host and Favorite Talk Show; 2012, Favorite Daytime TV Host

Genesis Awards (The Humane Society of the United States): 2009 (two awards), Best Talk Show and Gretchen Wyler Award (shared with Portia de Rossi); 2011, Best Talk Show

Woman of the Year (PETA): 2009

Teen Choice Awards: 2010, Choice Comedian; 2011, Choice Comedian

TV Guide Award: 2011, Favorite Host

FURTHER READING

Periodicals

Entertainment Weekly, Feb. 2, 2007, p.96; Jan. 15, 2010, p.26

Good Housekeeping, Oct. 2003, p.130; Oct. 2011

Hollywood Reporter, Feb. 23, 2007, p.O12

Newsweek, Sep. 15, 2008, p.103

People, Sep. 19, 2011, p.176

Publishers Weekly, Sep. 26, 2011, p.59
Redbook, Jan. 2006, p.88
Teen People, Feb. 2006, p.46
Time, Feb. 23, 2004, p.8
USA Today, Jan. 8, 2010

Online Articles

www.biography.com
   (Biography, "Ellen DeGeneres,"no date)
ellen.warnerbros.com/about/bio.php
   (Ellen DeGeneres Show, "Ellen DeGeneres Bio,"no date)
www.nytimes.com/pages/topics
   (New York Times, Times Topics, "Ellen DeGeneres,"multiple articles, various dates)
www.people.com/people/ellen_degeneres/0,,,00.html
   (People, "Ellen DeGeneres,"no date)

ADDRESS

Ellen DeGeneres
The Ellen DeGeneres Show
PO Box 7788
Burbank, CA 91522
ATTN: Fan Mail

WEB SITE

ellen.warnerbros.com

Drake 1986-

Canadian-American Rapper and Actor
Creator of the Hit Records *Thank Me Later* and *Take Care*
Played Jimmy Brooks on "Degrassi: The Next Generation"

BIRTH

Aubrey Drake Graham, known professionally as Aubrey Graham and also as Drake, was born on October 24, 1986, in Toronto, Ontario, Canada. His mother, Sandi, is a Canadian teacher. His father, Dennis, is an African-American musician from Memphis, Tennessee. As the son of an American and a Canadian, Drake has dual citizenship. This means that he is a citizen of both the U.S. and Canada.

YOUTH

Drake's parents divorced when he was five years old. His mother raised him in the Jewish faith of her family. He grew up celebrating Jewish holidays and had a *bar mitzvah* when he was 13 years old. (A *bar mitzvah* is a Jewish ceremony that formally marks the age at which a Jewish male assumes the responsibilities of observing the Jewish faith. It typically includes a religious ceremony and a party in the young man's honor.)

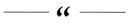

> "At the end of the day, I consider myself a black man because I'm more immersed in the black culture than any other," Drake commented. "Being Jewish is kind of a cool twist. It makes me unique."

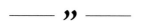

Drake grew up dividing his time between two very different worlds. For most of the year, he lived with his mother in an upper-class Jewish neighborhood in Toronto. As the only biracial person in the community, he often felt like an outsider. Summer vacations were spent with his father, aunts, uncles, and cousins in Memphis. Drake explored the Memphis music scene and often went to gigs with his musician father. Though Drake was very close to his mother, he felt more at home with his father's side of the family. "At the end of the day, I consider myself a black man because I'm more immersed in the black culture than any other," he commented. "Being Jewish is kind of a cool twist. It makes me unique."

EDUCATION

Drake attended Forest Hill Collegiate Institute in Toronto. He was often the only black student in his classes at school and sometimes had difficulties with other students because of that. "Going to Forest Hill was definitely an interesting way of growing up," he acknowledged. "When you're young and unaware that the world is made up of different people, it is tough growing up. But me being different from everyone else just made me a lot stronger."

Drake became interested in acting when he was young, working occasionally as a child model during elementary school and participating in his

A cast shot from "Degrassi: The Next Generation,"
with Drake in the front in a wheelchair.

high school's drama program. During high school, he was known for making people laugh. The father of one of his classmates was an acting agent, and he invited Drake to audition. He landed his first acting job when he was 14 years old, a small role in the 2002 movie *Conviction*. As an actor, he was known by his full name, Aubrey Graham.

This role led to Drake being cast in the Canadian teen drama series "Degrassi: The Next Generation." This television show was part of a series of popular and respected shows that had appeared on Canadian television, first "The Kids of Degrassi Street" (1979-1986), then "Degrassi Junior High" (1987-1989), followed by "Degrassi High" (1989-1991). The Degrassi shows followed the lives of a group of kids who lived on or near Degrassi Street in Toronto, Canada. Episodes of "Degrassi Junior High" and "Degrassi High" often included controversial subject matter, including teen sexuality, AIDS, teen pregnancy, abortion, drug abuse, racism, and teen suicide. TV critics applauded the Degrassi lineup, calling it "a series that dispenses with tidy morality and goes for the gut" and "a tough, compelling slice of life." Ten years after the end of "Degrassi High," the creators developed a new series, "Degrassi: The Next Generation," which focused on the stories of a new group of teens. When he was 16 years old, Drake dropped out of high school to begin filming "Degrassi: The Next Generation."

CAREER HIGHLIGHTS

"Degrassi: The Next Generation" began airing in the U.S. and Canada in 2001. The plot of the show focused on the lives of a group of students at

Degrassi Community School. Weekly episodes followed the experiences, challenges, and adventures of the group as they dealt with high school life. Drake played Jimmy Brooks, a wealthy, well-liked star player on the school's basketball team. In 2002, he and his "Degrassi: The Next Generation" costars won the Young Artist Award for Best Ensemble in a TV Series (Comedy or Drama).

During the fourth season of the series, as part of a storyline about school violence, Drake's character Jimmy is shot in the back by another student. Permanently injured by the shooting, Jimmy begins to use a wheelchair. Basketball was an important part of Jimmy's life, but he can no longer play on the school team. As the story develops, Jimmy must learn to adjust to new limitations in his abilities as he discovers who he is without sports to define him. In an interview shortly after the episode in which his character was shot, Drake said, "I took it very seriously. I spent a lot of time with someone in a wheelchair, and I also have a friend who had been shot. Playing Jimmy all day and being able to get up and walk away is weird; I appreciate things a lot more now."

Becoming a Rapper

While he was filming "Degrassi: The Next Generation," Drake had also been writing and recording his own raps in his spare time. "The reason it was rap was because in my mind I told myself, 'you're not a good enough singer,'" he admitted. "My father, actually, was always like, 'you've got a great tone … man, you gotta sing.'" Drake had appeared as an actor under the name Aubrey Graham. To keep his creative interests separate, he decided to use only his middle name to identify himself as a rapper. He recorded and released a series of mix tapes under the name Drake and sometimes using the nickname Drizzy Drake.

Drake released his first mix tape, *Room for Improvement,* in 2006. This collection of tracks featured guest performances by well-known artists who were also Drake's friends, including Trey Songz, Lupe Fiasco, and the Clipse. In 2007, Drake released *Comeback Season,* his second mix tape. Trey Songz appeared once again as a guest performer and was featured on the single "Replacement Girl."

Drake posted his mix tapes on his web site as free downloads. As people began to listen to his tracks, word spread quickly among music fans. Soon his mix tapes were being downloaded at a record-breaking pace. This attracted the attention of professionals in the music and entertainment industry. "Replacement Girl" was featured on BET's "106 & Park" program as

Drake performing with his mentor, Lil Wayne, in 2009.

a Joint of the Day, giving Drake a huge amount of exposure. He also received a 2008 BET Award for Best Male Hip-Hop Artist.

Around this time, the producers of "Degrassi: The Next Generation" became aware of Drake's growing success as a rap artist. During the final season of the series, a plot twist was written in to the show to have his character Jimmy writing and performing his own rap songs. All of Jimmy's raps were written by Drake.

Breakout Success

In 2008, Drake captured the attention of rap superstar Lil Wayne. A friend had given Lil Wayne a copy of one of Drake's mix tapes. After listening to the first few tracks, Lil Wayne invited Drake to fly to Houston for a meeting. The result of that meeting was Drake's 2009 mix tape, *So Far Gone.*

With another round of guest performances by well-known rap artists, including Lil Wayne, *So Far Gone* became an instant sensation. The single "Best I Ever Had" reached No. 1 on the *Billboard* Hot R&B/Hip-Hop Songs chart. Drake won two Juno Awards in 2008, one for Best New Artist and another for Rap Recording of the Year for *So Far Gone.* This was an amazing accomplishment for Drake, an independent artist with no recording contract who was giving his music away for free on the Internet. Seemingly overnight, he went from underground rapper to mainstream recording artist.

Drake left "Degrassi: The Next Generation" in 2009 when his character graduated from high school. Soon after, he signed a recording contract with Lil Wayne's Young Money Entertainment label. Around that time, he also went on tour with Lil Wayne. This gave Drake the opportunity to perform in front of thousands of fans. He attracted new fans at every show and his mix tapes became even more popular.

In late 2009, Drake released an EP version of his mix tape *So Far Gone.* It debuted at No. 6 on the U.S. *Billboard* 200 chart. Drake won two *Billboard* Music Awards in 2009. He won the *Billboard* Top New Hip Hop/R&B Artist Award and the Top Rap Song Award, for "Best I Ever Had." BET also honored Drake with two awards in 2009: he was named the BET Hip-Hop Rookie of the Year and also received the BET Hip-Hop Track of the Year Award for his single "Every Girl."

Drake was nominated for two 2010 Grammy Awards for *So Far Gone* and performed with Lil Wayne and Eminem on the Grammy Awards TV broadcast. This caused a stir in the music industry because he had not yet released an official studio album. At that time it was completely unprecedented for an artist to be recognized with Grammy nominations for a mix tape. Though Drake did not win a Grammy that year, his appearance on the TV broadcast set the stage for his first major record release.

Thank Me Later

Drake released his debut album *Thank Me Later* in 2010. This highly anticipated album featured collaborations with such rap superstars as Kanye West, Jay Z, and Lil Wayne. On the day the record was released, Drake planned to give a free concert in New York City. When more than 25,000 fans showed up, things quickly got out of control. The New York City police department cancelled the concert because the unruly crowd was too large for the location.

Thank Me Later was a phenomenal hit with music fans and critics alike. With *Thank Me Later*, Drake introduced a new style of hip-hop that blended rap and R&B singing styles. According to *Billboard* magazine contributor Mariel Concepcion, "As hip-hop continues to drift further away from rap's basic elements and seeks to re-energize and expand its fan base with a new, hybrid sound that blends rap, R&B, dance, even alt-rock … this half-singing, half-rapping, half-Jewish, half-black former actor and current heartthrob is helping change the face of the genre firsthand."

The success of *Thank Me Later* brought Drake more in touch with mainstream music listeners. As Kelley L. Carter wrote in *Jet*, "Drake isn't exactly the archetype emcee. He's less

"Drake isn't exactly the archetype emcee. He's less about bling and more about interesting wordplay.… You won't find him talking much about illegal activities in his music. Instead, you'll find him making humorous, clever digs at popular culture and addressing his love of the ladies and how he's handling his newfound fame."
—*Kelley L. Carter*, Jet

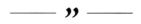

about bling and more about interesting wordplay. He doesn't exactly know what it's like to walk on the seedier side of life, so you won't find him talking much about illegal activities in his music. Instead, you'll find him making humorous, clever digs at popular culture and addressing his love of the ladies and how he's handling his newfound fame." *Washington Post* music reviewer Chris Richards said, "He's tugging on a strand of pop music that feels both magical and rare—the kind that brings us all together by reminding us that we're all alone." Drake ended 2010 with a performance on "Dick Clark's Rockin' New Year's Eve" TV program, broadcast to viewers around the world. In 2010, Drake received the BET Hip-Hop MVP Award and was also named Man of the Year by *GQ* magazine.

In 2011, Drake received the BMI Urban Award for Songwriter of the Year and the Hal David Starlight Award from the Songwriters Hall of Fame. Also in 2011, he appeared on "Saturday Night Live" where he performed his single "Make Me Proud" with Nicki Minaj. Sales of "Make Me Proud" skyrocketed in the weeks after the program aired. During the "Saturday

Drake performing with Nicki Minaj on "Saturday Night Live," 2011.

Night Live" episode, Drake also performed in several comedy sketches. He later said that being on "Saturday Night Live" made him want to return to acting. "I caught that acting bug again," he admitted. "I'm dying to be on sets and be part of some movies. So hopefully I'll find some time for that amidst all the touring. It was nice to show people in those skits that I can get out of rapper mode and just be funny."

Take Care

Drake released his second album, *Take Care,* in 2012. This record included tracks that were more introspective and emotional than his previous recordings. On this album he once again used a blend of rapping and singing, and the track lyrics gave listeners a glimpse into his private life. *Take Care* was almost like a musical version of his diary, as he rapped and sang about romance, the downside of fame, and his feelings about specific events in his life.

"Music is the only way that I can really vent and tell my story. It's definitely personal. It's definitely very vivid, detailed, and I feel it's an incredible chapter of my life documented. All these albums and mix tapes are just time markers for me. Pictures and social media are great, but I think the best way for me to remember real feelings that I've experienced is to make music about it," Drake said. "I always feel that with each new project, a new group of people are dying to see what my next move is. With that comes pressure, but it also creates excitement and makes me want to work harder. I still feel that I am new and I have something to prove with this album."

Take Care was received warmly by fans and critics, who praised Drake's ability to cross musical genres with ease. *New York Times* music reviewer Jon Caramanica wrote, "*Take Care* isn't a hip-hop album or an R&B album so much as an album of eccentric black pop that takes those genres as starting points, asks what they can do that they haven't been doing, then attempts those things. In the future an album like this will be common-place; today, it's radical." Also writing in the *New York Times*, Nate Chinen said, "Rapping well, singing even better and erasing distinctions between the two, Drake made the sleekest, most self-aware pop album of the year."

Drake's rapid rise to fame seemed to surprise even the most seasoned music industry professionals. As Benjamin Meadows-Ingram wrote in *Billboard*, "In his short career, he's already appeared on the *Billboard* Hot 100 with 30 different songs and cracked the top ten seven times, the best performance by any rapper in the chart's history besides Lil Wayne, who's tallied 49 songs on the chart and eight top tens." *Take Care* received a 2012 Juno Award for Rap Recording of the Year.

Other Plans

Drake has managed to remain grounded even as his reputation and success as an artist continue to grow. "My life has changed, but I have a great grasp on it," he pointed out. "By no means have I paid my dues yet. But I think I've put in enough work where people understand that I'm here to stay." His future plans include more acting projects—he appeared as a voice actor in the 2011 video game *Gears of War 3* and the 2012 animated movie *Ice Age: Continental Drift.* Drake also plans to develop a line of personal fragrances and scented products for the home, including candles and incense. *Fame: Drake*, a comic book about Drake's life, was published in 2012.

Though he has earned his reputation as a talented songwriter and recording artist, Drake is sometimes still surprised by his own success. "I'm accepted by fans, accepted by my peers. It's crazy. The images that exist of me pre-2007 are, like, horrendous, like Phat Farm velour suits, big afro, like, it's terrible. So just the fact that the world allowed me to grow—I grew up in

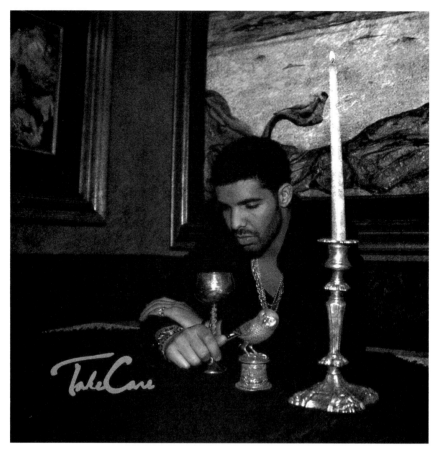

Take Care, *Drake's second album, showed his growth as an artist.*

front of the world and they watched it, and now they want to hear my story," Drake said. "I get respect from the guys who are respected for being real rapper's rappers. I get respect from women. I get respect from mothers, fathers, and kids. It's very humbling and flattering and incredible, and I'm honored to be in this position because I get to be myself. And I get a lot of love for it."

Still, Drake acknowledged that "Real, legendary status can't be dictated by the people who are still here witnessing it. Legendary status is when the next generation comes up. The kids that are 15 right now and will be going to college in five or six years—if they say, 'Yo, I remember when Drake came to this school. That's one of the most legendary shows ever,' that's when you're a legend. I'm young. I'm 23. This is too soon. I really want to grow and be that guy."

"I want to encourage my generation to love, to be happy. I want to encourage open communication. And even though it's not always a good thing—some things are better kept to yourself—but I want to encourage my generation to be honest, to be yourself. If you don't like doing drugs or you don't want to fight people in the street, it's OK. That's never been cool anyway. To me, losers do that. It's way cooler to be yourself. If you're good at math, be good at math. If you're good at acting or drama, just be you. Just be what you're good at."

HOME AND FAMILY

When he is not travelling or on tour, Drake divides his time between homes in Toronto and Miami, Florida.

SELECTED CREDITS

"Degrassi: The Next Generation," 2001-2009 (TV series)
Room for Improvement, 2006 (mix tape)
Comeback Season, 2007 (mix tape)
So Far Gone, 2009 (mix tape)
So Far Gone, 2009 (EP)
Thank Me Later, 2010 (album)
Take Care, 2012 (album)

HONORS AND AWARDS

Young Artist Award: 2002, Best Ensemble in a TV Series (Comedy or Drama) for "Degrassi: The Next Generation"
BET Hip Hop Award: 2008 (two awards), Best Male Hip-Hop Artist and Best Group; 2009 (two awards), Rookie of the Year and Track of the Year, for "Every Girl"; 2010, MVP Award
Juno Award: 2008 (two awards), Best New Artist, and Rap Recording of the Year, for *So Far Gone*; 2012, Rap Recording of the Year, for *Take Care*
Billboard Music Award: 2009 (two awards), Top New Hip Hop/R&B Artist, and Top Rap Song, for "Best I Ever Had"
GQ Award (*GQ*): 2010, Man of the Year
BMI Urban Award: 2011, Songwriter of the Year
Hal David Starlight Award (Songwriters Hall of Fame): 2011

FURTHER READING

Periodicals

Billboard, May 29, 2010, p.20; Nov. 19, 2011
Ebony, Mar. 2010, p.38

Jet, Sep. 20, 2010, p.28; Dec. 5, 2011, p.22
Maclean's, June 22, 2009; June 28, 2010, p. 44; Jan. 16, 2012
Newsweek, Nov. 21, 2011
Rolling Stone, Aug. 2, 2009, p.31; Sep. 30, 2010, p.30
USA Today, Nov. 17, 2011
Wall Street Journal, Nov. 11, 2011
Word Up!, Jan. 2011, p.28

Online Articles

www.billboard.com/#/artist/drake/855020
  (Billboard, "Drake,"no date)
www.biography.com/people
  (Biography, "Drake,"no date)
www.cbc.ca/archives
  (CBC Digital Archives, "The Degrassi Approach to Children's Drama,"
  no date)
www.kidzworld.com
  (Kidz World, "Drake Biography,"May 8, 2012)
www.mtv.com/music/artist/drake/artist.jhtml
  (MTV, "Drake,"no date)
www.rollingstone.com
  (Rolling Stone, "Artist to Watch 2009: Drake,"Aug. 7, 2009; "Drake,"
  Sep. 29, 2010)

ADDRESS

Drake
Universal/Republic
1755 Broadway, 8th floor
New York, NY 10019

WEB SITE

www.drakeofficial.com

Kevin Durant 1988-

American Professional Basketball Player
Forward for the Oklahoma City Thunder

BIRTH

Kevin Wayne Durant was born in Suitland, Maryland, on September 29, 1988. His mother, Wanda (Durant) Pratt, is a postal worker, while his father, Wayne Pratt, works as a federal law enforcement officer with the Library of Congress. At the time of Kevin's birth, his parents were unmarried, so he was given his mother's maiden name. His father was not involved in his upbringing for most of his childhood. Instead, his mother raised him and his older brother, Tony, as a single mom with the help of his grandmother, Barbara Davis. Durant's parents reunited and married in 2001. "My wife did a tremendous job with those boys," Wayne Pratt explained in the *Dallas Morning News*. She is the rock and the strength of our family." Durant has two brothers, Tony and Rayvonne, one sister, Briana, and a stepbrother, Cliff Dixon.

YOUTH

Kevin grew up in the Suitland-Silver Hill area of Prince George's County, Maryland, just outside Washington DC. During his elementary school years, he participated in a range of after-school sports at the Boys & Girls Club program in Capitol Heights, including playing lineman on the football team. A hard worker with natural athletic ability, he was also a thoughtful and respectful young boy. His mother told the *New York Times* about a football practice during which the coach challenged a less-athletic teammate to tackle him. After the practice, Kevin revealed to his mother that he had let his teammate tackle him—had purposely risked his own humiliation—to save the young teammate from being bullied. "'Mom, he couldn't knock me down,'" he confessed. "'I let him knock me down because I didn't want anybody to hurt him.'"

"It was tough," Durant said about his training regime. "I didn't like it at all, I wanted to play with my friends. [Coach Brown] told me that I would pick up bad habits by playing 5-on-5, so every day I just did the drill work. It was like boot camp every day. It made me cry all the time—I just told myself not to be a quitter."

Kevin and his brother Tony spent a lot of time at the Seat Pleasant Activity Center near his grandmother's house. Kevin joined the PG Jaguars, an Amateur Athletic Union (AAU) youth basketball team, and played alongside future Minnesota Timberwolves forward Mike Beasley. According to Beasley, the Jaguars were the "best nine-year-old team in Prince George's County." As Beasley told the *Minneapolis Star Tribune,* "That jump shot Kevin's got? Kevin's had that his whole life. Every time I grabbed a rebound, I'd just throw it out to Kevin." Beasley's mom would take Mike to Kevin's house in the mornings. They would eat breakfast, ride the bus, and play basketball after school together. "I love him like a brother," Durant said as he reflected on Beasley's success in the NBA. "We worked so hard.... Playing each other on the highest stage of basketball is an unbelievable feeling. It's just a blessing."

Durant was a quiet boy with a vivid imagination. His mother recalled that he was always capable of entertaining himself, often disappearing into a corner of his grandmother's house to play. "It was just a penny and a clothespin," she told the *Washington Post*. "That's what he was playing with. And he'd spend hours … just sitting there, playing with a penny and a clothespin."When she asked him what he was doing, he told her that he was making up basketball plays. Around that same time, when Durant was nine or ten years old, he greatly admired NBA player Vince Carter of the Toronto Raptors. His mother bought him a Vince Carter uniform that he insisted on wearing to all of his games. "I always wanted to play the way he did, so I would always want to wear his uniform," he explained. "I still call myself a big Vince Carter fan."

At age 11 Durant knew he wanted to be a professional basketball player. He told his mother about his dream after a big game with the Jaguars—a tournament final—in which he scored 18 points in the second half to secure the championship for his team. "I don't know if she thought I was serious or not," Durant admitted, "but she said, 'All right, if that's what you want, then you've got to work hard and commit to it.'" AAU coach Taras Brown agreed to train him, and the two began meeting daily to practice drills that would improve his form, agility, strength, accuracy, and endurance. Durant recalls sprints up and down steep hills and long afternoons in the gym doing hundreds of laps, crab-walk exercises, and drills to hone his shooting, dribbling, passing, and defensive skills. He lovingly refers to Brown as his godfather, and he credits him with shaping his dream into a reality. Brown was a strict coach, however, forbidding Durant from playing in pickup games on the playground so that he could focus on technique. He also challenged him by making him write essays on basketball and diagram the mechanics involved in a jump shot. Brown's motto was "Hard work beats talent when talent fails to work hard."

From age 11 to age 16, Durant trained with Brown for several hours every day. His routine consisted of attending school, completing his homework, running to the gym, and then working out late into the evening. His grandmother would bring his dinner to the gym and he would scarf it down between drills. Training for a basketball career required extraordinary mental and physical discipline. "It was tough," Durant admitted. "I didn't like it at all, I wanted to play with my friends. He told me that I would pick up bad habits by playing 5-on-5, so every day I just did the drill work. It was like boot camp every day. It made me cry all the time—I just told myself not to

Durant was a basketball prodigy even in high school, the MVP of the McDonald's High School All-American Game, 2006 (shown here).

be a quitter." In retrospect, he has said that "Honestly, I don't know how I did all of those things when I was younger. I just wanted to be great."

EDUCATION

Durant spent his freshman and sophomore years of high school at National Christian Academy in Fort Washington, Maryland, playing point guard on the junior varsity team before being upgraded to the varsity team midway through his freshman season. During his sophomore year he became the team's leading scorer, playing guard, forward, and center. He led the team to 27 victories, a school record. His National Christian coach, Trevor Brown, described him as both modest and driven. "He was never a kid who needed to play in front of big crowds, who needed to be a star, who needed all the accolades," he told the *Washington Post*. "That's not him. He was always more concerned with being the best player possible."

For his junior year, Durant attended Oak Hill Academy in Mouth of Wilson, Virginia, a school renowned for its basketball program. He started in every game, helping the team advance to the national championship with a 34-2 record. For his senior year, he transferred to Montrose Christian Academy in Rockville, Maryland, to play on the team of Stu Vetter, a seasoned coach who had trained multiple future NBA players and had led many high school teams to the national championships. Durant took an hour-long train ride every morning to school, and then at 7:30 a.m. he fit in a 45-minute workout before the beginning of the school day. After afternoon basketball practice ended, he would stay 45 minutes for additional training. As Durant approached graduation, he was getting attention as one of the top high school players in the nation, averaging 23.6 points and 10.2 rebounds per game. He received handwritten letters from college coaches and was named the 2006 All-Met Player of the Year by the *Washington Post*. He also earned Most Valuable Player honors for his performance in the 2006 McDonald's High School All-American Game.

Meanwhile, Durant remained active in AAU basketball at Seat Pleasant Activity Center. During his high school years, he played on the DC Blue Devils alongside future Denver Nuggets point guard Tywon Lawson. Coaches with the Blue Devils have described Durant as a likeable teen with a positive attitude who achieved success through old-fashioned hard work. He was particularly close to his AAU coach and mentor Charles Craig, whom he affectionately called "Big Chuckie." Coach Craig, he has stated, taught him "how to be tough, how to go out there and play with passion and play with heart." In April 2005, however, when Durant was a junior in high school, Craig was murdered at the age of 35. "I didn't know what to think," Durant lamented. "He's a person that died for no reason." Since Craig's death, Durant has worn the number 35 in tribute to him. "He was just a caring and loving person that everybody would love to meet," he said. "Every time I step on that floor, I do it to win games and make him proud."

As the annual NBA draft approached, Durant was considered the number-two recruit in the nation in the class of 2006. That year, however, the NBA increased the age requirement from 18 to 19, requiring players to play at least one year beyond high school before being eligible for the NBA draft. Multiple colleges attempted to recruit him, but Durant chose the University of Texas because of his respect for coaches Russell Springman and Rick

Texas Longhorns player Durant (35, left) goes for a rebound against Oklahoma Sooners player Nate Carter (24, right), 2007. Durant won multiple major awards for his performance at the University of Texas.

Barnes. He moved to Austin and began preparing for his freshman season with the Longhorns. Many predicted that he would enter the NBA draft after just one year of college ball, but he was reluctant to declare himself a one-year-and-out student athlete, focusing instead on the hard work ahead of him in the classroom and on the court.

To the delight of his parents and coaches, Durant excelled at the university both academically and athletically. He became a two-time member of the

University of Texas Athletics Director's Honor Roll, which requires a minimum 3.0 grade point average, and cited his anthropology course as a favorite class. He enjoyed learning about different cultures around the world, both past and present. "The rituals of how they found food were just amazing to me," he remarked. "They had to catch it, cook it, make sure it's not poisoned—all that different type of stuff."

At the same time, Durant participated in what he refers to on his website as "one of the greatest seasons in the history of college basketball." He set records in both scoring and rebounds in the Big 12 college athletic conference, averaging 25.8 points and 11.1 rebounds per game. He also set the University of Texas record for total points and total rebounds in a single season. Coach Rick Barnes called him the best player in the history of the Longhorns, citing his versatility and spot-on instincts. Durant earned the Most Valuable Player Award for the Big 12 conference and was named National College Player of the Year by the National Association of Basketball Coaches, the U.S. Basketball Writers Association, *Sporting News,* and the Associated Press (AP). He also won three major awards for outstanding college basketball player of the year—the Adolph Rupp Trophy for NCAA basketball player of the year, the Naismith Award, and the John R. Wooden Award—and was the first freshman in NCAA history to win any of those awards. Despite this recognition, he maintained his humility, declining to pose for the cover of *Dime* magazine unless the other four starting Longhorns were pictured alongside him. He was also selected to appear on the cover of the March Madness 2008 video game.

CAREER HIGHLIGHTS

The Seattle Sonics

In June 2007 Durant started his professional career when he was chosen by the Seattle SuperSonics as the second overall draft pick. Ohio State University player Greg Oden was selected as the first pick by the Portland Trailblazers, but Durant's supporters believed that he deserved top billing. As coach Barnes told the *Dallas Morning News,* "Kevin's the best player in the draft—period, at any position." Durant's father agreed, telling the *Seattle Times,* "You haven't seen anything yet. He's prepared almost his entire life for this and he's only going to get better." But Durant shied away from claims that he would save the Seattle franchise. "I don't think I'm the face of the franchise like everybody has been saying," he stated. "I don't think I'm going to be the star. I just want to play within the flow of the team."

Members of the press and professional basketball community had high expectations for Durant, who at age 19 was the youngest player in the NBA.

———— **"** ————

"If you would have told me a couple of years ago that I would be the NBA Rookie of the Year, to be in the same company as LeBron James, Larry Bird ... I would have told you you were crazy," Durant said in amazement.

———— **"** ————

Despite his humble demeanor, he was an intimidating addition to the league. "His length, his height,"Timberwolves Coach Kurt Rambis marveled in the *Star Tribune,* referring to Durant's six-feet, nine-inch frame and wingspan of seven feet, five inches. Fran Blinebury of the *Houston Chronicle* lauded his diverse skill set and ability to transcend the requirements of a single position. "If Durant were a restaurant, he'd be an all-you-can-eat buffet, where the only things that matter are appetite and imagination," Blinebury wrote. "He has the splendid athleticism of the greatest small forwards and brings guard skills that boggle the mind. He has an impressive shooting range and the height, wingspan, and shot-blocking ability of a center."Sportswriter Jerry Brewer of the *Seattle Times* echoed these comments. "Don't characterize him as either a small forward or power forward. Just consider him, as many experts do, a prodigy capable of redefining how we label players."From his first day as a Sonic, Durant expressed his willingness to work hard to live up to their expectations. "I'll play all five positions if my team needs me to,"he said. Sonics Coach P. J. Carlesimo likened his enthusiasm to that of Magic Johnson and Michael Jordan when they were his age, while others compared him to Hall of Fame scoring champion George Gervin.

Durant made his NBA debut on October 31, 2007, in a game against the Denver Nuggets. Although the Sonics lost, Durant made a solid first impression with 18 points, five rebounds, and three steals. On November 16, 2007, during his tenth professional game, he scored his first game-winning basket—a three-pointer in double overtime—to beat the Atlanta Hawks. "Every game I play in, it's like I'm star-struck," he said during his rookie season. "But once the ball is tipped, you've got to get all that out of your mind. It's fun playing against the best players in the world."Durant averaged 20.3 points per game, becoming the third teenager in the history of the NBA with a per-game scoring average above 20. He was the only rookie to lead his team in five different categories: points, blocks steals, free throws made, and free throw percentage. He also blocked more shots than any other guard in the league. He was selected as a member of the NBA All-Rookie First Team and was named Rookie of the Year, the first Sonics player to receive this honor. "If you would have told me a couple of years

*In his rookie season in the NBA, Durant may have been a little
starstruck by some of his superstar opponents, including
Grant Hill (shown here) of the Phoenix Suns.*

ago that I would be the NBA Rookie of the Year, to be in the same company as LeBron James, Larry Bird … I would have told you you were crazy,"
he said in amazement. Always one to keep his success in perspective, he
said, "I just can't be complacent with just making it. I've got to keep working and keep getting better."

Unfortunately, Durant's scoring and shot-blocking record could not elevate the Sonics' reputation in 2007-2008. They ended the season with 20 wins and 62 losses, the second-worst record in the NBA. "[To] lose at something you love so much, at something you work so hard at, that makes it that much harder. We didn't lose much when I was at Texas, or in high school or in AAU, so it is not something I am used to.... The guys in our locker room fight so hard in games and work so hard in practice. But you have to take your lumps to become great." Despite the team's losses that year, Durant rose in fame and popularity, signing endorsement deals with Nike, the videogame developer EA Sports, and Gatorade.

The Oklahoma City Thunder

In July 2008, the Sonics announced their relocation to Oklahoma City, Oklahoma, where they were renamed the Thunder. Durant was in Austin taking summer classes at the University of Texas when the announcement was made. "I thought we would be [in Seattle] for at least two more years," he stated. "I got a phone call—the team is moving to Oklahoma City, this year, now. I was shocked." During the Thunder's inaugural 2008-2009 season, Durant ranked sixth in the NBA for scoring, averaging 25.3 points per game despite spending eight games on the sidelines due to an injury. In February 2009 he returned to the University of Texas for a ceremony in which officials retired his No. 35 jersey. "It was really emotional," Durant recalled. "[The No. 35] represents one of my closest friends, my AAU coach, Charles Craig.... It means more than just my jersey number hanging up in the rafters. It is everything he's done for me in my life, everything he did to help ... the kids who played for him.... My coach is going to be up there forever." That same month, he earned MVP honors in the Rookie/Sophomore T-Mobile Challenge after scoring 46 points. His impressive performance captured the attention of commentators, who began calling him by the nickname "Durantula."

In summer 2009, Durant again returned to his college campus to take classes toward a degree in education, a dream he says he plans to accomplish no matter how many summers it takes. In addition to studying, he spent the summer doing strength training and defensive drills in preparation for his third year in the NBA. His hard work paid off during the 2009-2010 season, when he led the Thunder in steals and averaged 30.1 points per game to become the NBA's scoring champion. At age 21, Durant was the youngest player ever to earn this distinction. He was selected for the Western Conference All-Star team in 2010, and he enjoyed a scoring streak of 25 or more points in 29 consecutive games. He capped off the season by leading the Oklahoma City Thunder to the playoffs with a 50-32 record.

Durant drives against the Minnesota Timberwolves in 2010,
when he led the league in scoring.

Although the Thunder lost to the Los Angeles Lakers in the first round of the postseason, Durant earned NBA Western Conference Player of the Month honors for April.

In July 2010, Durant signed a five-year contract extension worth $86 million with the Thunder. "I just told everybody I wasn't talking about it, really. I just kept it to myself. That's just the type of person I am. I don't like the attention around me," he said of the low-profile deal. Considering his scoring performance, the deal received very little hype and fanfare in the press, which Jack McCallum of *Sports Illustrated* attributed to the fact that Durant is "seemingly uncorrupted by what we consider the me-first culture of the

NBA." In his fourth season with the Thunder, he led the NBA in scoring and was named to the All-NBA First Team for the second year in a row. Fans voted him to the NBA Western Conference All-Star Team for a second time, this year as a starting player. The Thunder won 55 games during the regular season and advanced to the Western Conference Finals before being defeated by the Dallas Mavericks.

The International Spotlight

Durant was chosen to play on the U.S.A. Basketball team for the 2010 FIBA World Championship tournament. "He's the whole package," explained U.S.A. Basketball's Managing Director Jerry Colangelo in the *New York Times.* "This is his opportunity to come forth on an international stage." Seizing that opportunity, Durant led his team to victory over Turkey in the finals, securing the world championship title for the U.S.A. for the first time since 1994. "My only option was to come out here and get a gold, and it feels really good to bring this back to the States," he said. He claimed the Most Valuable Player award for his solid performance throughout the tournament, especially the final three games in which he scored 33, 38, and 28 points against Russia, Lithuania, and Turkey, respectively. Overall, he averaged 22.8 points and 6.2 rebounds per game, propelling the undefeated Team U.S.A. to its World Championship gold-medal finish and paving their way to the 2012 Olympics.

During the summers of 2010 and 2011, Durant traveled to China as a spokesperson for Nike Basketball. There he participated in basketball clinics, charity events, and Nike store appearances while meeting his fans overseas. In July 2011 he joined a star-studded team of NBA players in the Philippines for a pair of exhibition games to benefit the MVP Sports Foundation. Meanwhile, NBA owners and the players' union were in the midst of a lockout because they could not reach a new collective bargaining agreement. The stall in labor negotiations delayed the start of the 2011-2012 NBA season by two months and reduced the number of games from 82 to 66. Late in the summer of 2011, Durant considered opportunities to play basketball in Turkey, Spain, and Russia before turning instead to the Hollywood spotlight. That September, when he would ordinarily be preparing for training camp, he began filming a Warner Brothers movie. The yet-to-be-released *Thunderstruck* is a family-friendly basketball comedy about a klutzy young fan who magically switches talents with Kevin Durant—his hero—to become the star of his high school team. Durant, meanwhile, cannot make a basket to save his life.

The 2011-2012 season presented yet another opportunity for Durant to shine. On February 19, 2012, he scored a career-best 51 points in a game against the Denver Nuggets. The crowd chanted "MVP!" as he made two free throws in the final seconds of the game to solidify the Thunder's 124-118 win. A week later he played in his third NBA All-Star game. He scored 36 points and grabbed seven rebounds to usher the Western Conference team to a 152-149 victory, a performance that earned him the All-Star MVP award. By the end of the regular season he had improved his game in several areas, setting career highs in assists per game (3.5) and rebounds per game (8.0), and improving his defense. For the third year in a row, he was the NBA scoring champion, averaging 28 points per game. "If Durant hasn't fully come into his own, the rest of the NBA should really be afraid. He can already do it all," wrote commentator Sean Gregory in *Time*.

That spring, Durant ushered the Thunder into the postseason, carrying the team to victory over the Dallas Mavericks, the Los Angeles Lakers, and the San Antonio Spurs in the playoffs. The Thunder than faced LeBron James and the Miami Heat in the 2012 NBA Finals. As the press analyzed the exciting matchup between star players Durant and James, they predicted that it could blossom into the NBA's next great rivalry. "A new era in the NBA arrived at long last, and it took two men to deliver it," Ian Thomsen wrote in *Sports Illustrated* as the Finals began. "[James and Durant] are the seminal players of this post-Kobe era, and each is seeking his first title at the other's expense. The last Finals to launch a new generation with so much anticipation and promise was the showdown of the Lakers and the Celtics in 1984, when Magic Johnson succumbed to Larry Bird over seven memorable games....

"[James and Durant] are the seminal players of this post-Kobe era, and each is seeking his first title at the other's expense," Ian Thomsen *wrote in* **Sports Illustrated.** *"Neither Durant nor James can know for sure what the other is capable of accomplishing in this series, because they've never put each other to the ultimate test. And so the new era begins."*

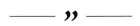

Durant is a naturally ruthless finisher, a closer who is every bit as mean in the final minutes as he is nice off the court. James is at heart a playmaker who was blessed with the physical gifts of Michael Jordan yet desired instead to fulfill his own egalitarian vision of Magic creating for himself and others. Lately, the two have been trying to emulate each other's games: Durant has become a better defender and passer as well as OKC's leading re-

Durant chasing LeBron James in the 2012 NBA Championships,
which Miami won four games to one.

bounder, while James has shown more willingness to hunt for his shot in the game's final minutes rather than play the playmaker."

"These Finals defy prediction,"Thomsen continued. "In its initiation of a rivalry that has been long anticipated, there is no history from which to draw. Neither Durant nor James can know for sure what the other is capable of accomplishing in this series, because they've never put each other to the ultimate test. And so the new era begins." Unfortunately for Durant and the Thunder, the series did not live up to the hype. The Thunder won Game 1 105-94, but then went on to lose the next four games in a row. Durant turned in an excellent performance, averaging 30.6 points a game in the Finals while shooting 54.8 percent from the field, but James was un-stoppable. Oklahoma City lost the championship to Miami in Game 5.

The 2012 Olympics

Durant was selected as part of the U.S. basketball team for the 2012 Olympic Games, held in London, England. The U.S. team was made up of professional players from many different NBA teams, giving the athletes the chance to play with their usual rivals while representing the United States. The U.S. team was expected to dominate the competition, and it did. In the preliminary round, a series of 5 games, the U.S. knocked out each of their rivals, beating France 98-71; Tunisia 110-63; Nigeria 156-73; Lithuania 99-94; and Argentina 126-97. The game against Nigeria was perhaps their easiest win, a blowout in which the U.S. set an all-time Olympic scoring record. The game against Lithuania was by far their toughest battle, with Lithuania answering every U.S. score with one of their own. With the USA trailing 82-80 in the fourth quarter, LeBron James scored 9 of his 20 points in the last 4 minutes to help the team outlast Lithuania.

With their undefeated record, the U.S. moved on to the quarterfinals as the No. 1 seed. The team faced Australia, which put up a tough contest. Durant managed five 3-pointers during the 42-point third quarter and helped the team take control during the second half. He shot 8-of-10 3-pointers to lead the team with 28 points, helping the U.S. defeat Australia 119-86. The U.S. then advanced to the semifinals against Argentina. Once again 3-pointers were a big factor. With the U.S. leading by seven points at halftime, Durant sank two 3-pointers in an 8-0 run in the third quarter that gave the team some breathing room, and then sank 2 more to help the team take a 74-57 lead into the fourth quarter. He finished with 19 points, and the U.S. knocked out Argentina 109-83 to advance to the gold medal game.

The gold medal game was seen as a rematch of the final game of the 2008 Beijing Olympic game against Spain. It was an exciting, hard-fought game that featured 16 lead changes and 6 tied scores. According to the AP, "This was no Dream Team. This was reality. The gold medal was in doubt for the U.S. men's basketball team. The Americans led Spain by only one point after three quarters, a back-and-forth, impossible-to-turn-away-from game that almost anyone would hope for in an Olympic final." Durant scored 30 points and led a balanced attack that helped the undefeated U.S Olympic Men's Basketball Team fight off Spain for a 107-100 win to capture the Olympic gold medal. Durant's 30-point game tied the third-highest total in U.S. Olympic history. He grabbed 9 rebounds and shot 5-of-13 3-pointers to set a U.S. Olympic single-game record for 3-pointers attempted. He also drew 9 Spanish fouls to finish 9-of-10 from the free throw line.

"They are a tough team," Durant said about the Spanish team. "They made it tough for us all night. Fourth quarter, we were able to pull away, make some big shots. We have so many weapons on this team that can take over a game, but everybody chipped in tonight, and we got a really good win." And not just a win—an Olympic gold medal. "I have a gold medal," he ex-

*U.S. players Durant (left), Carmelo Anthony (center left),
LeBron James (center right), and Kobe Bryant (right)
pose with their gold medals at the 2012 Olympics in London, England.*

claimed. "It's unbelievable, man. I couldn't sleep last night waiting for the game. I'm glad we came out and got the W."

After the game, Durant talked about his time at the Olympics. "I put everything aside. I put the NBA season aside," he said. "I just wanted to come out here and play my role for this team. I had a great year. A really fun year. I'm so blessed to be healthy and play the game that I love every day. I could have been at home working out, but I was here, fighting for my country, and it's a great feeling."

During the eight Olympic games, Durant led Team USA in scoring with 156 total points (19.5 points per game) and was second in rebounding with 46 total offensive and defensive rebounds (5.8 rebounds per game). He also had a team-high five blocks. His 156 total points in the Olympic tournament set a new U.S. record and inspired a lot of praise. "As potent a scorer as Durant was last NBA season—he led the league with 28 points a game—he was even more deadly in the Olympics," Robert Klemko wrote in *USA Today*. "He set a Summer Games record with 34 three-pointers, shooting 52% from beyond the arc in London. A prolific shot-maker in those playoffs, Durant took on a new identity early in the Games, passing up shots to get his well-decorated peers involved. On a team stacked with scorers, Durant stressed unselfishness, and then teammates started begging him to shoot."With this new style of play, many commentators looked forward to the next NBA season to see if Durant can continue his outstanding Olympic play and turn it into an NBA championship.

In spite of his quick ascent to the top, Durant is still described by his coaches and fellow players as humble, loyal, and down to earth. As former NBA coach Jeff Van Gundy told *Time,* "I have no question that with his work ethic, and sense of team, Durant is going to go down as one of the greatest of the greats in the NBA."When asked about the future, Durant stated, "I just see myself as a good pro, a great vet who helps a lot of guys out, and a champion."

HOME AND FAMILY

Durant shares a close bond with his mother, whom he credits with teaching him the importance of a strong work ethic. "I can't explain how important my mom is in my life,"he said. He has respect for the hard work she did when he was a boy, working the midnight shift to make ends meet for their family. While his mom was at the post office, he spent time with his grandmother, with whom he is also very close, and his mother's sister, Aunt Pearl, who died of breast cancer when he was 11. To honor his aunt's memory, he scribbles "Aunt Pearl" on his sneakers. He recently worked with Nike on a special-edition shoe, the Nike Zoom KD IV "Aunt Pearl,"as a tribute to her. The sneaker features a hidden inscription that reads "In memory of Aunt Pearl, who inspired us all to continue the fight for a cure."

When Durant signed with the Seattle Supersonics, his mother moved to Mercer Island, Washington, so she could cook for him and help him gain weight. "She can make me a better person and make the transition easier, so why not,"he reasoned. He recently purchased a home in the upscale Gaillardia section of Oklahoma City, which he shares with his brother Tony and his dogs, Diego and Capone. His parents, though frequent visitors to Oklahoma City, maintain their permanent residence near Washington DC. When Durant scored a career-best 51 points in early 2012, his family members were courtside to celebrate. "They've been there with me ever since I was eight trying to play this game,"he said. "To score 50 points with them on the sideline at the highest level of basketball is a dream come true and a blessing."

HOBBIES AND OTHER INTERESTS

Although Durant is a self-proclaimed basketball fanatic, he also has a passion for music. An aspiring music producer and sound engineer, he has a home studio where he spends time rapping and mixing music. In addition to making music, he enjoys playing video games like "NBA Live" and "March Madness." He also likes to shop for clothes and has unexpectedly become a style icon for sporting black-rimmed glasses, a plaid button-up dress shirt, and his signature accessory—the backpack—in which he keeps a bible, sneakers, headphones, his iPad, and other gadgets. After he created a buzz by wearing the book bag into his press conferences in 2011, Nike announced a new line of limited edition Kevin Durant backpacks that were an instant hit.

Durant is known for interacting with his fans via social media. He has more than one million followers on Twitter. On October 31, 2011, four months into the NBA lockout, he tweeted, "Anybody playing flag football in [Oklahoma City]? I need to run around or something." Oklahoma State University student George Overbey responded by inviting Durant to an intramural game that evening. A few messages later, Durant was on his way to campus to pick up Overbey at his house and drive him to the football field. "I think people were skeptical that he was actually going to come. I was trying to keep it as low-key as I could. But that didn't work so well," Overbey explained in *Tulsa World*. Playing quarterback, Durant threw four touchdowns, and he picked off four passes while playing defense. "He's such a good, quality guy. It's just unbelievable to see someone that successful, that admired to be so humble," Overbey said. "It really is incredible. It speaks volumes about his character." Attendees of the game described Durant as patient and generous as he posed for photos and signed autographs after the game.

In addition to being an all-star on the court, Durant has established himself as a community leader with a generous heart and boundless energy. He has hosted numerous charity events, teaches kids in a summer basketball Pro-Camp in Oklahoma City, and has taught youth basketball clinics all over the country. He returns home to the Washington DC area as much as he can and has given back to his hometown community by funding major renovations at his old childhood hangout, the Seat Pleasant Activity Center.

HONORS AND AWARDS

Adolph Rupp Trophy: 2007, for NCAA basketball player of the year

John R. Wooden Award (Los Angeles Athletic Club): 2007, for the outstanding college basketball player in the United States

Naismith Award (Atlanta Tipoff Club): 2007, for men's college player of the year

NCAA Division 1 Player of the Year (National Association of Basketball Coaches): 2007

Oscar Robertson Trophy (U.S. Basketball Writers Association): 2007, for NCAA basketball player of the year

Player of the Year (*Sporting News):* 2007

Player of the Year (Associated Press-AP): 2007

Rookie of the Year Award (National Basketball Association): 2007-2008

T-Mobile Rookie Challenge Most Valuable Player Award: 2009

FIBA World Championship Most Valuable Player Award (International Basketball Federation): 2010

All-Star Game Most Valuable Player Award (National Basketball Association): 2012

Olympic Men's Basketball: 2012, gold medal (with USA Men's Olympic Basketball Team)

FURTHER READING

Books

Doeden, Matt. *Kevin Durant: Basketball Superstar,* 2012 (juvenile)

Sandler, Michael. *Kevin Durant,* 2012 (juvenile)

Savage, Jeff. *Kevin Durant,* 2012 (juvenile)

Periodicals

Current Biography Yearbook, 2010

Men's Fitness, Nov. 2009, p.33

New York Times, Dec. 13, 2007, p.D4; July 8, 2010, p.B13; Aug. 15, 2010, p.SP5; Sep. 13, 2010, p.D2

Seattle Times, July 1, 2007

Sporting News, Mar. 30, 2009, p.40; Aug. 17, 2009, p.80; June 21, 2010, p.22; June 6, 2011, p.15

Sports Illustrated, Feb. 19, 2007; Nov. 12, 2007, p.52; Dec. 24, 2007, p.72; Sep. 20, 2010, p.12; June 18, 2012

Washington Post, Aug. 15, 2011, p.D6

Online Articles

www.espn.com
(ESPN, "Kevin Durant Splits from Longtime Agent," Feb. 17, 2012; "Kevin Durant Wins All-Star Game MVP," Feb. 26, 2012; "Kevin Durant, U.S. Pull through in Final as Spain Can't Rain on Parade," Aug. 12, 2012)

www.chron.com
(Houston Chronicle, "Stock Is Soaring: The Skinny on Kevin Durant," June 26, 2007)

sportsillustrated.cnn.com
(Sports Illustrated, "Phenomenal Freshman," Feb. 19, 2007; "The Kid Enters the Picture," Nov. 12, 2007; "All Hail a King without the Bling,"

Sep. 20, 2010; "Immune to Hype, Humble Durant Following His Own Path to Greatness," June 13, 2012; "Let the Rivalry Begin," June 18, 2012; "Durant, James Lead USA Past Spain 107-100 for Hoops Gold Medal," Aug. 12, 2012)

www.time.com

(Time, "Q&A: Kevin Durant on NBA Draft Day," June 28, 2007; "How Team USA Won Men's Hoops—and the Entire Olympics," Aug. 12, 2012)

www.usatoday.com

(USA Today, "Durant Scores 51 as Thunder Top Nuggets in OT," Feb. 19, 2012; "Thunder Top Lakers, Tie Miami as NBA's Best," Feb. 24, 2012; "Durant Earns MVP Honors," Feb. 27, 2012; "Kevin Durant Drops 38, Thunder Beat Magic," Mar. 1, 2012; "USA Men Survive Spain to Win Basketball Gold Medal" and "Durant Sinks Shots, Spain in Finale," Aug. 12, 2012)

ADDRESS

Kevin Durant
Oklahoma City Thunder
Two Leadership Square
211 North Robinson Ave., Suite 300
Oklahoma City, OK 73102

WEB SITES

kevindurant35.com
www.nba.com/playerfile/kevin_durant

Zaha Hadid 1950-

Iraqi-Born British Architect and Designer
First Female Winner of the Pritzker Prize,
Architecture's Highest Honor

BIRTH

Zaha Hadid was born on October 31, 1950, in Baghdad, Iraq.
Her father, Muhammad Hadid, was an economist, business-
man, and politician who co-founded the progressive Iraqi National Democratic Party. Her mother did not work outside the
home, but raised Hadid and her two brothers: Haytham, 15
years older, and Foulath, 12 years older.

YOUTH

When Hadid was a child, during the 1950s and early 1960s, Iraq was different than it is today. At that time Iraq was a modern, liberal country with a secular, Westernized outlook. Hadid's father had studied at the London School of Economics and was involved in progressive politics, serving as Iraq's Minister of Finance in the late 1950s. Hadid was an active child, "asking questions all the time," she recalled. Although her family was Muslim, Hadid attended a convent school in Baghdad, where her fellow students came from various religious backgrounds. She grew up believing there were few limits to what a girl could achieve. "There was never a question that I would be a professional," she recalled. For a time she wanted to become a singer, and she also considered becoming a politician or a psychiatrist.

> *Hadid grew interested in historic architecture when her father took her to visit the ancient cities of Sumer. "I was amazed," she recalled. "We went by boat, and then on a smaller one made of reeds, to visit villages in the marshes. The beauty of the landscape—where sand, water, reeds, birds, building, and people all somehow flowed together—has never left me."*

It was design and architecture that claimed her imagination. "Architecture was used as part of nation-building in Iraq then," Hadid said of her childhood, and "I saw this great modern architecture every day." Her school sat across from a building designed by Italian architect Gio Ponti, while her family owned one of the earliest Iraqi houses built in the Bauhaus fashion, a modernist style that emerged from Germany in the 1920s and 1930s. Her aunt built a modern house in northern Iraq, and Hadid was nine when her father took her to an exhibition that featured it. Afterwards, she recalled, "I became obsessed by the topic." She also grew interested in historic architecture. Her father took her to visit the ancient cities of Sumer, which flourished over 4,000 years ago in what is now southern Iraq. "I was amazed," she recalled of the trip. "We went by boat, and then on a smaller one made of reeds, to visit villages in the marshes. The beauty of the landscape—where sand, water, reeds, birds, building, and people all somehow flowed together—has never left me." She was 11 or 12 when she decided she wanted to be an architect.

Hadid in her London office, 1985.

EDUCATION

Hadid completed her secondary education at a boarding school in Switzerland, then entered the American University of Beirut, Lebanon. She received her Bachelor of Science degree (BS) in mathematics in 1971, and the following year she moved to London, England, to study at the Architectural Association (AA). Her instructors there supported experimental design, but also insisted she master draftsmanship, the art of drawing architectural plans. Hadid graduated in 1977, receiving the school's Diploma Prize for her graduation portfolio. The portfolio featured a striking design for a 14-story hotel on London's Hungerford Bridge, in the middle of the River Thames. One critic later said of the design: "It really was one of these very rare moments when a fissure opens up in architecture, and a different way of seeing emerges. We no longer have to be bound by gravity. We don't have to accept reality—she will unfold her own reality."

CAREER HIGHLIGHTS

A Frustrating Start

Today, Zaha Hadid is a world-renowned architect known for her influential and revolutionary structures. She struggled for years to achieve success, however. Her early career was marked by building plans that people admired but would not construct, and it took two decades before her designs were in demand.

After Hadid completed her architecture degree in 1977, she was invited by one of her instructors, Dutch architect Rem Koolhaas, to join his company, the Office of Metropolitan Architecture. Koolhaas would eventually design award-winning buildings around the world. He was linked with architecture's "deconstructivism" movement, which emphasized unusual shapes, such as curves or jagged lines, over more traditional rectangular shapes. Hadid's designs were also in the deconstructivist tradition; they were rendered as oil paintings that were impressionistic, with an emphasis on unusual shapes and shadows that seemed to move fluidly. The curves of Arabic calligraphy and intricacies of Persian carpet patterns also influenced her architectural ideas. Sometimes her designs were so abstract that people who saw them doubted they could be translated into real buildings.

In 1980, Hadid left the Office of Metropolitan Architecture to found her own practice in conjunction with the AA. She spent the next decade or more establishing and building her practice. To support herself, she also taught architecture at the AA and later lectured at Harvard University, the University of Illinois, and Yale University. In 1982 she beat more than 500 other entrants to win her first design competition, for Hong Kong's Peak Leisure Club. Her design, a "horizontal skyscraper" that featured four huge beams that looked as if they were emerging from a mountainside, was never built. Nevertheless, her designs were catching international attention; they were exhibited in New York, Tokyo, and London, including shows at the Guggenheim Museum in 1978 and the Museum of Modern Art in 1988. In 1987 she established Zaha Hadid Associates in London and soon hired her long-time business partner, Patrik Schumacher. Some of her early work included interior design work for apartments in London and a restaurant in Sapporo, Japan, as well as several temporary art installations. Her interior work also included designing furniture. In 1989, Hadid became a British citizen.

In 1993, Hadid finally completed her first building project, a fire station for the Vitra Furniture Company in Weil am Rhein, Germany. The Vitra Fire Station showcased a sharply angled roof that resembled a wing in flight. Large glass windows set into angled concrete walls put the fire engines on display. The client was thrilled with the completed design, noting that Hadid was his first choice "because we felt that her architectural vision was very dynamic, daring, and also evinced danger." After a few years, however, Vitra's fire company was moved to another facility, and the building was turned into a museum.

*The Vitra Fire Station in Weil am Rhein, Germany, was
Hadid's first completed building project.*

In 1994, Hadid seemed to have broken through with a winning design for
the Cardiff Bay Opera House, in the capital city of Wales in the United
Kingdom. Her design called for a glass courtyard to surround the auditori-
um. The design took spectacular advantage of the waterfront site, but public opinion turned against the project. Critics called the design too modern
and elitist for a construction project funded by lottery money. The local
government decided to build a stadium instead. Hadid believed her background as a foreign-born woman created resentment toward her design.
"When I was in Cardiff they didn't talk to me. Literally. They looked at me
sideways, or behind me. Not all of them, but some quite specific people,"
she recalled. "I don't know whether people responded to me in a strange
way because they just thought I was one of those eccentric people, or they
thought I was a foreigner or behaved funny or I'm a woman." The debacle
in Cardiff seemed to confirm her reputation as an architect who created interesting designs but could not turn them into real buildings.

Pushing the Boundaries of Building

At first the Cardiff rejection made Hadid believe her career was over, but
she was able to change her attitude. "I made a decision that I wasn't
going to be bitter," she explained. "And you know what? It made us
tougher as a practice." During the 1990s, advances in computer-aided design made it easier for her striking designs to be translated into workable
building plans. In the latter part of the decade Hadid continued teaching
and submitting designs to competitions. As technology caught up to her

———— " ————

*"[The Rosenthal Center] is
an amazing building, a work
of international stature that
confidently meets the high
expectations aroused by this
prodigiously gifted architect,"
Herbert Muschamp stated.
"Might as well blurt it out:
the Rosenthal Center is the
most important American
building to be completed
since the end of the
cold war."*

———— " ————

imagination, more of her projects reached the construction stage. In 2001, her design for a combination tram station and parking lot, the Hoenheim-Nord Terminus and Car Park, was completed in the city of Strasbourg, France. The design made use of parallel lines—angular columns in the terminus, perfectly cylindrical lights, even the lines to designate parking spaces—to create a sense of overlapping fields knitted together into a whole. The result resembled a forest, something growing organically from the site. The project earned the Mies van der Rohe Award, the European Union's Prize for Contemporary Architecture.

Hadid was also honored for a project completed in 2002, the Bergisel Ski-Jump and Lodge in Innsbruck, Austria. The former host city of the Winter Olympics decided to upgrade their ski jump on Bergisel Mountain and selected a design by Hadid that incorporated spaces for public facilities, including a café and viewing terrace. At 295 feet long and almost 165 feet high, the new facility was part tower, part bridge, and its sinuous shape led some to nickname it the "Cobra." The cobra's "head," comprising both the public spaces and the top of the jump, provided spectacular views of the surrounding Alps mountain range. The design won awards from both regional and national governments of Austria, as well as a Gold Medal for Design from the International Olympic Committee.

In 2003, Hadid completed her first building in the United States, the Lois and Richard Rosenthal Center for Contemporary Art, in Cincinnati, Ohio. The building was the first major American museum to be designed solely by a woman and made the most of its relatively small space on a city corner. The exterior was an irregular arrangement of blocks made from concrete and translucent glass. The interior used concrete as well, continuing the outside sidewalk into a concrete path that curved into the wall, creating an "urban carpet" that connected the interior spaces. Combined with an atrium and staircases that played with vertical space, the interior created a sense of movement that invited visitors into the variously sized exhi-

The Lois and Richard Rosenthal Center for Contemporary Art in Cincinnati, Ohio.

bition galleries. "It is an amazing building, a work of international stature that confidently meets the high expectations aroused by this prodigiously gifted architect for nearly two decades," architecture critic Herbert Muschamp stated in the *New York Times*. "Might as well blurt it out: the Rosenthal Center is the most important American building to be completed since the end of the cold war." The building earned Hadid the International Award from the Royal Institute of British Architects (RIBA), her first recognition from this respected group.

The recognition helped Hadid feel more accepted by the architectural community, but awards were not the goal of her work. "No matter how many prizes you get, you are still walked all over by your clients,"she commented. "It's a very tough profession, and so it brings you down to earth." Instead, Hadid worked to inspire imaginations through her designs. "People don't want to be in the kind of space that they inhabit every day,"she explained. As her career developed, she had to combat the pressure of always being new and innovative. "There's a point when you have to try to always be inventive—out of that you do discover things that you would have never thought possible. On the other hand, you have to build on your repertoire and make it fresh in different ways." One common thread she saw in her work was "the connection between project and site."Tailoring each project to fit within its environment—city corner, factory site, urban center—made her work very interesting.

Earning the Prestigious Pritzker Prize

Hadid had completed only a few projects during her early career, but she was widely acknowledged as having a great influence on modern architecture, through both her designs and her teaching. In 2004, the jury for the Pritzker Architecture Prize, architecture's equivalent to the Nobel Prize, selected Hadid to receive the honor. In their announcement, the jury noted, "Clients, journalists, fellow professionals are mesmerized by her dynamic forms and strategies for achieving a truly distinctive approach to architecture and its settings. Each new project is more audacious than the last and the sources of her originality seem endless."Hadid felt particularly gratified by the award, which she was the first woman to receive. "I think it shows that you can actually break through the glass ceiling," she said. Although she didn't want to be thought of as a "woman architect," she added that she was glad to be a role model for up-and-coming women in the field. "When I lecture all over the world, women come up to me all the time to tell me how encouraged they are."

After winning the Pritzker Prize, Hadid's practice grew even faster. Her staff increased rapidly—from five people in 1985 to more than 300 in 2010—and the firm was able to complete more buildings. In 2005 she finished two buildings in Germany, the Phaeno Science Center in Wolfsburg and the BMW Central Building in Leipzig. The Phaeno Science Center resembled a massive three-sided concrete boulder, pocked with irregularly shaped windows, while the interior had curving floors like sand dunes. The BMW Central Building was part of a campus that included three factories, and her design called for the assembly line to travel through the central management building. Rubberized pathways on the floor were included to

The MAXXI Museum for XXI Century Art in Rome, Italy—a view of the main entrance showing stairways and bridges.

resemble roadways and encourage movement within the building. "Our work has always been influenced by ideas of movement," Hadid noted of the design. "There's always a desire to achieve buildings with fluidity and complexity." Office cubicles were open to outside areas, and company executives noted that communications between factory workers and management increased after the building opened. The BMW building earned a prize from the German government, while both of Hadid's German buildings won the RIBA Europe Award.

By this point Hadid had worked around the world, but not in her adopted country. She had become a British citizen in 1989 and had been recognized in 2002 with a Commander of the British Empire honor. Despite her growing international reputation, however, it was not until 2006 that she completed her first building in the United Kingdom. That project was relatively small, a Maggie's Cancer Care Centre in Fife, Scotland. Some critics attributed Hadid's slow path to acceptance in Britain to her reputation as a diva, someone who can be difficult to work with. The architect herself admitted that "I don't have the patience, and I'm not very tactful. People say I can be frightening." Another explanation, she suggested, was that her designs tended to be radical and intimidating. "In another way, I can be my own worst enemy," she explained. "As a woman, I'm expected to want everything to be nice, and to be nice myself. A very English thing. I don't design nice buildings—I don't like them. I like architecture to have some raw, vital, earthy quality." Despite the potential for culture clash, Hadid chose to stay in Britain throughout her career to take advantage of the country's rich tradition of skilled engineers, an important factor in realizing some of her designs.

Gaining World Renown

In 2009, Hadid completed her largest project to date, the 30,000-square meter (almost 323,000-square foot) MAXXI Museum for XXI Century Art in Rome, Italy. Her design called for a "confluence of lines" to blur the boundaries between indoor and outdoor spaces; winding lines of concrete, steel, and glass moved and intersected to draw in the visitor. *New York Times* architecture critic Nicolai Ouroussoff noted that "its sensual lines seem to draw the energy of the city right up into its belly, making everything around it look timid.… The idea is to weave her buildings into the network of streets and sidewalks that surround them—into the infrastructure that binds us together. But it is also a way of making architecture—which is about static objects—more dynamic by capturing the energy of bodies charging through space." Ouroussoff added that the museum "will only add to [Hadid's] legacy." In 2010, the MAXXI Museum earned Hadid RIBA's highest honor, the Stirling Prize for building of the year, as well as the RIBA Europe Award.

"[Hadid's] recent buildings have proved a revelation, confounding her critics and cementing her reputation … as one of the very few who are genuinely attempting something new," wrote Edwin Heathcote. "Her buildings are fluid, theatrical and sculptural—structurally daring and spatially inventive, they sweep you up and astound you."

In 2010 Hadid also completed her first permanent structures in Asia and the Middle East. The Guangzhou Opera House became a feature of Guangzhou (formerly known as Canton), China's third largest city. The building contained an exterior featuring a multitude of triangular windows as well as ramps and staircases that connected performance spaces to plazas, a reflecting pool, and the park outside it. Hadid's design won the RIBA International Award. *New York Times* critic Ouroussoff called the building "the most alluring opera house built anywhere in the world in decades.… [The design] establishes the opera house and its grounds as part of the public realm—something that belongs to

The Riverside Museum:
Scotland's Museum of Transport and Travel in Glasgow, Scotland.

everyone, not just elite opera fans." Another work completed in 2010, the Sheikh Zayed Bridge, was a wavelike structure connecting Abu Dhabi Island to the mainland of the United Arab Emirates. The curved design of the arches is said to evoke sand dunes in the desert.

By the time she turned 60 in 2010, Hadid was widely acknowledged as one of the world's preeminent architects. "Her recent buildings have proved a revelation, confounding her critics and cementing her reputation not only as the world's foremost female architect but also as one of the very few who are genuinely attempting something new," Edwin Heathcote wrote in the *Financial Times*. "Her buildings are fluid, theatrical and sculptural—structurally daring and spatially inventive, they sweep you up and astound you."

In 2011 Hadid completed a smaller but still celebrated project: the Evelyn Grace Academy in Brixton, a lower-income neighborhood of London. Her design used sleek lines and a Z-shape to integrate classrooms and athletic fields, while still dividing the building into four sub-schools. The architect felt very strongly that interesting, beautiful buildings should be available to everyone. "Part of architecture is about making people feel good in their space," she noted, especially in areas where people may not have many resources. "It's important to think about architecture in a way that inspires people in their locale—because not everyone is privileged enough to travel the world and see the great wonders." The Evelyn Grace Academy earned Hadid her second Stirling Prize for building of the year as well as the RIBA London Award.

The Evelyn Grace Academy was the first in a run of completed projects in Hadid's adopted country. "Something has changed radically here recently," she noted. "There is no resistance to the new any more. Eventually this will filter through into building. England being part of Europe is the most positive thing that could have happened." In 2011, another unique Hadid design opened in the United Kingdom, the Riverside Museum: Scotland's Museum of Transport and Travel. The building featured an irregular zigzag of a roof, which resembled a river and echoed the corrugated roofs of Glasgow's old industrial sheds. The design encouraged a sense of motion—ideal for a transport museum—and helped tie together the building with its surroundings. That year Hadid also completed first major commission in England, the London Aquatics Centre. Her design resembled a wave or sea creature and was the most notable structure completed for the Olympic Games of 2012.

Bringing Design to the World

In 2012, Hadid's firm had projects under construction all over the world. These included an art museum on the campus of Michigan State University; a spiral tower in Barcelona, Spain; a museum and cultural center in Baku, Azerbaijan; an office and retail complex in Beijing, China; and an oyster-shaped ferry terminal in Salerno, Italy. In 2012 she also signed a contract to design the new Iraq Central Bank, her first building for her native country of Iraq.

Hadid has maintained a busy schedule as head of a globally influential architecture firm but has also continued devoting time to lecturing and edu-

Hadid at the opening of her art exhibit at the Design Museum in London, 2007.

cation. She served as a professor at the University of Applied Arts in Vienna, Austria, and often lectured at conferences and exhibitions. She herself was the focus of retrospective exhibitions at New York's Guggenheim Museum in 2006, London's Design Museum in 2007, and the Pallazzo della Ragione in Padua, Italy in 2009. Her work was also made part of the permanent collections at New York's Museum of Modern Art and the German Architecture Museum (Deutches Architektur Museum). Hadid has earned numerous honorary doctorates and fellowships, including membership in the American Institute of Architects and the American Academy of Arts and Letters, and she was named a United Nations Education, Scientific and Cultural Organization (UNESCO) Artist for Peace in 2010.

In addition to designing buildings, Hadid has occasionally dabbled in interior and fashion design. She has created handbags, shoes, furniture, vases, wallpaper, shelving units, and cutlery. "For an architect, everything connects," she explained. "The design of a handbag, or furniture, or cutlery have their challenges, and they're fun to do. I'd love to get some designs into mass, low-cost production. I want to be able to touch everyone, not just the educated and cultural elite, with a little of what we can do. One of the things I feel confident in saying we can do is bring some excitement, and challenges, to people's lives. We want them to be able to embrace the unexpected." Hadid has said that she creates her designs "so that people can experience things they wouldn't otherwise. Whether it's a good school, or a nice museum, or a concert hall, or having a nice street or street furniture or a lamp, I think all these things need to be very inspiring."

HOME AND FAMILY

Hadid, who has never married, has made her home in London since moving there in the early 1970s to study architecture. She owns the top floor loft in a five-story building, and it is decorated with her own paintings and furniture designs. She spends time with her brother Foulath, a historian at England's Oxford University, and his family. As of 2012 she had not returned to her childhood home of Iraq since 1980—most of the people she knew growing up left the country during its various wars over the past 30 years. She looked forward to a possible return to her native country after signing a contract in 2012 to design the new Central Bank of Iraq.

HOBBIES AND OTHER INTERESTS

As the head of a busy architectural firm, Hadid has had precious little free time for hobbies, often working late into the night on her projects. Nevertheless, she has always been interested in style and fashion—her own personal style extends to a fondness for wearing capes—and occasionally she designs wearable items for various fashion companies. Her work has included an experimental handbag for Louis Vuitton; limited edition shoes for Lacoste; and necklaces, rings, and cuffs for Swarovski crystal. In 2008, she designed a traveling exhibition space for noted fashion company Chanel, at the request of head designer Karl Lagerfeld.

SELECTED WRITINGS

Zaha Hadid: The Complete Buildings and Projects, 1998, 2nd ed., 2009
Zaha Hadid: Thirty Years of Architecture, 2006 (with Detlef Martins and Patrik Schumacher)
Zaha Hadid: Complete Works, 2009

HONORS AND AWARDS

Commander of the Order of the British Empire: 2002
Austrian State Architecture Prize: 2002, for Bergisel Ski Jump
Mies van der Rohe Award-European Union Prize for Contemporary Architecture (European Commission/Fundació Mies van der Rohe): 2003, for Hoenheim-Nord Terminus and Car Park
International Award (Royal Institute of British Architects): 2004, for Lois & Richard Rosenthal Center for Contemporary Art; and 2011, for Guangzhou Opera House
Pritzker Prize for Architecture (Hyatt Foundation): 2004
Europe Award (Royal Institute of British Architects): 2005, for BMW Central Building; 2006, for Phaeno Science Centre; 2008, for Nordpark Railway Stations; and 2010, for MAXXI Museum
Deutscher Architekturpreis-German Architecture Award (German Architecture Association): 2005, for BMW Central Building
Thomas Jefferson Foundation Medal in Architecture (Thomas Jefferson Foundation and University of Virginia): 2007
Praemium Imperile (Japan Art Association): 2009
Stirling Prize (Royal Institute of British Architects): 2010, for MAXXI Museum; and 2011, for Evelyn Grace Academy
Artist for Peace (United Nations Education, Scientific and Cultural Organization—UNESCO): 2010
Commandeur de l'Ordre des Arts et des Lettres (Republic of France): 2010, for services to architecture
London Award (Royal Institute of British Architects): 2011, for Evelyn Grace Academy
Global Road Achievement Award for Design (International Road Federation): 2012, for Sheikh Zayed Bridge

FURTHER READING

Periodicals

Architectural Digest, Oct. 2004, p.110
Architectural Record, Aug. 2005, p.82; Oct. 2010, p.82
Architectural Review, Aug. 10. 2011
Building Design, Feb. 4, 2005, p.8
Current Biography Yearbook, 2003
Financial Times (London), June 29, 2002, p.7; May 25, 2004, p.13; Oct. 17, 2006, p. 10; June 30, 2007, p.15
Guardian (England), Oct. 8, 2006
Interview, Feb. 2005, p.132
New York Times, June 8, 2003, p.1; Mar. 28, 2004; June 2, 2006; Nov. 12, 2009; July 5, 2011
New York Times Magazine, May 16, 1993, p.33
New Yorker, Dec. 21, 2009, p.112; July 24, 2011, p.80
Newsweek, May 19, 2003, p.78; Sep. 26, 2011, p.52
Progressive, June 2008, p.33
Time, Apr. 29, 2010
Times (London), May 16, 2009, p.3

Online Articles

www.guardian.co.uk/artanddesign
    (Guardian, England, "Space Is Her Place,"Feb. 1, 2003)
www.pritzkerprize.com/laureates/2004
    (Pritzker Architecture Prize, "Zaha Hadid: 2004 Laureate,"accessed
    April 2, 2012)
www.scotsman.com
    (Scotsman, Edinburgh, "Interview: Zaha Hadid, Architect Who Builds
    the Unbuildable,"June 9, 2011)
www.telegraph.co.uk/culture/art/architecture
    (Telegraph, England, "Zaha Hadid's Fantastic Future,"Jan. 1, 2012)

ADDRESS

Zaha Hadid Architects
10 Bowling Green Lane
London EC1R 0BQ
United Kingdom

WEB SITE

www.zaha-hadid.com

Josh Hutcherson 1992-

American Actor

Starred in *Bridge to Terabithia, Journey to the Center of the Earth,* and *The Hunger Games*

BIRTH

Joshua Ryan Hutcherson was born on October 12, 1992, in Union, Kentucky. His father, Chris, works as an analyst for the Environmental Protection Agency. His mother, Michelle, worked for Delta Airlines. He has a younger brother named Connor who is also an actor.

YOUTH AND EDUCATION

Hutcherson knew at a very young age that he wanted to become an actor, though he does not remember exactly when he first had the idea. "I just kind of wanted to do it," he explained. "I felt like this was what I was meant to do." At first, his parents resisted the idea. They thought their son was too young to make a decision like that. "Being from Kentucky, you know, you don't really know much about the business," he acknowledged. "You hear all of the negative connotations that come with the words 'child star' and 'child actor.' They kind of wanted to keep me out of all that stuff. They just wanted me to keep on playing T-ball, but you know, I was ready to move on from T-ball."

> "
>
> *Hutcherson knew at a very young age that he wanted to become an actor, but his parents thought he was too young. "Being from Kentucky, you know, you don't really know much about the business," he acknowledged. "You hear all of the negative connotations that come with the words 'child star' and 'child actor.' They kind of wanted to keep me out of all that stuff. They just wanted me to keep on playing T-ball, but you know, I was ready to move on from T-ball."*
>
> "

A few years passed and Hutcherson still had not given up his dream of acting. His parents reconsidered the idea when he was eight years old and allowed him to try out during pilot season, the period when many television networks film the pilot episodes, the first episode of a new TV show. "An acting coach said we should go out to California for pilot season," Hutcherson recalled. "My mom had just taken a leave of absence from Delta Airlines, and we were so confused. We didn't know what a pilot was."

Hutcherson and his mother went to Los Angeles so that he could begin auditioning for acting jobs. By the time he was nine years old, he had hired his first acting agent. With the agent's help, he soon landed roles in TV commercials and also appeared in the pilot episode for a new TV show.

Hutcherson and his mother spent the next few years travelling between California and Kentucky. When he wasn't working, they lived in Kentucky with his family. The family also had an apartment in Burbank, California, where Hutcherson and his mother stayed when he was auditioning for roles or filming in the Los Angeles area.

Hutcherson provided the voice of Markl in Howl's Moving Castle.

By this point Hutcherson was beginning to develop a career as an actor, but as he explained, "I was still a kid. I still had a childhood. It was just a little bit different from a normal one." Whenever he was at home in Kentucky, he liked to be outdoors doing things like looking for snakes in the creek near his home and playing football and soccer. He also enjoyed playing Guitar Hero II with his brother. As a teenager, he liked to compete in triathlons. (A triathlon is a multi-sport event in which participants compete to finish three consecutive races in the shortest amount of time. Triathlons normally include swimming, biking, and running races.)

Between acting jobs Hutcherson attended Ryle High School in Union, Kentucky. Whenever he was working, he studied with a tutor.

CAREER HIGHLIGHTS

Hutcherson's first notable acting job was on a 2002 episode of the TV series "ER." His first movie role was in the 2003 made-for-TV movie *Wilder Days*. In this movie, he played Chris, a boy who goes on an adventurous road trip with his father and grandfather. After that, Hutcherson landed some parts as a voice actor. He provided the voice of Markl in the English-language version of the animated movie *Howl's Moving Castle*. Hutcherson was also the voice of one of many "Hero Boys" in the animated feature film

The Polar Express. By the time he started high school, he had already appeared in several movies and TV shows.

Hutcherson's first supporting role in a theatrical movie release was in the 2005 sports comedy *Kicking & Screaming*. He played Bucky, the son of demanding soccer coach Buck (played by Robert Duvall) and half-brother of Phil (played by Will Ferrell). Hutcherson's first starring role was as Gabe in the 2005 movie *Little Manhattan*. In this coming-of-age story, 11-year-old Gabe navigates a complicated family life and his first real crush on a girl.

Zathura

Hutcherson's first major role was in the 2005 adventure *Zathura*, based on the picture book by children's author Chris Van Allsburg. *Zathura* was a follow-up to *Jumanji*, also by Van Allsburg. In *Jumanji*, two children find an old board game and decide to play. They are transported into the most astonishing and frightening adventures, and they can't escape until they finish the game. At the end of the story, the children try to get rid of the game, but another child takes it home.

In *Zathura*, Walter (played by Hutcherson) and his brother Danny (played by Jonah Bobo) set off an unexpected chain of events when they decide to play the old board game, which was hidden in the basement of their new house. As the boys begin to play, events in the game come to life. A meteor shower destroys part of the house, killer robots and monsters appear, and the house itself goes flying through space. To set things right, the two brothers must figure out how to stop arguing with each other and work together as a team for the first time in their lives. According to *Entertainment Weekly* movie reviewer Scott Brown, "From a Hollywood that often settles for less in the family department, *Zathura* is a rarity: a stellar fantasy that faces down childhood anxieties with feet-on-the-ground maturity." Hutcherson won a 2006 Young Artist Award for Leading Young Actor for his portrayal of Walter in *Zathura*.

Bridge to Terabithia

Hutcherson next appeared in the 2007 movie *Bridge to Terabithia*, based on the Newbery Award-winning 1977 book by Katherine Paterson. Hutcherson played Jess Aarons, a talented artist who is an outsider at school and within his own family. Tormented by school bullies and his four sisters, and mostly ignored by his father, Jess is lonely and alone. Then he meets Leslie (AnnaSophia Robb), a new girl at school who soon becomes his best friend. Together Leslie and Jess create an imaginary forest kingdom called Terabithia. They begin spending most of their free time in Terabithia, which

Hutcherson with AnnaSophia Robb in a scene from Bridge to Terabithia, *adapted from the novel of the same name by Katherine Paterson.*

can only be reached by swinging across a creek on a rope that hangs from a tree. Jess and Leslie build a tree house where they make up fantastic stories about monsters and dangerous quests. Leslie helps Jess learn about courage, strength, and true friendship. These qualities prove invaluable to Jess when he must come to terms with a terrible tragedy that he feels responsible for causing.

"I read the book when I found out it was getting made into a movie … and as I was reading it, I could see it coming to life off the pages, and I could picture myself as Jess. Then I got the script, I read the script, I loved the script. And I was like, I just read this, I just read the book, it's the exact same thing pretty much. They kept it so true to the book," Hutcherson said. "I think that there are kids who are outcasts, and they get kind of picked on at school. They need to find a good friend to hang out with and create sort of a fantasy world, like we did in the movie."

Bridge to Terabithia earned good reviews from movie critics, as in this comment from *Hollywood Reporter* critic Michael Rechtshaffen: "The fantasy-adventure incorporates the novel's magical and emotional elements without overplaying either—a balance that hasn't always proven easy to maintain in the world of kid-lit adaptation." *New York Times* movie reviewer Jeannette Catsoulis praised *Bridge to Terabithia* as "a thoughtful and extremely affecting story of a transformative friendship between two unusually gifted children.… Consistently smart and delicate as a spider web, *Bridge to Terabithia* is the kind of children's movie rarely seen nowadays. And at a time when many public schools are being forced to cut music and art from the curriculum, the story's insistence on the healing power of a nurtured imagination is both welcome and essential." For his role in *Bridge to Terabithia*, Hutcherson won a 2008 Young Artist Award for Leading Young Actor.

Journey to the Center of the Earth

Hutcherson's next starring role was in the 2008 remake of the adventure story *Journey to the Center of the Earth*, an adaptation of the 1874 novel by French science fiction pioneer Jules Verne. *Journey to the Center of the Earth* was the first live action feature film produced in high-definition 3-D. In this movie, Hutcherson played Sean, whose father has disappeared mysteriously. Sean is sent to visit his uncle Trevor (played by Brendan Fraser), who is a geologist and volcanologist. In a box of his father's papers, Sean discovers a copy of the book *Journey to the Center of the Earth*. The book contains notes written by Sean's father showing that volcanoes could contain a way to reach the Earth's core. Uncle Trevor impulsively sets off with Sean to investigate this theory. In Iceland, Sean and Uncle Trevor team up with Hannah (played by Anita Briem), a mountain guide whose own father believed that it was possible to discover another world at the Earth's center. The team sets off for the mouth of a volcano and soon find themselves immersed in a fantastic and dangerous adventure travelling through the hidden world beneath the surface of the Earth.

Journey to the Center of the Earth was dismissed by most critics, though younger movie fans enjoyed the fast-paced special effects. Still, Hutcherson's performance as Sean increased his popularity with moviegoers and led to him being cast in more starring roles.

Hutcherson returned to the role of Sean in the 2012 adventure movie *Journey 2: Mysterious Island*. This sequel is based on the Jules Verne novel *The Mysterious Island*, published in 1874. This story follows Sean, now 17 years old, as he joins up with his new stepfather Hank (played by Dwayne Johnson) on a mission to find Sean's long-lost grandfather. After Sean and Hank intercept and decode a strange distress signal, they realize that Sean's grandfather may be stranded on a remote island in the South Pacific. They hire a pilot to fly them to the island, where they crash into a spectacular fantasy world where nothing is normal. While navigating many dangerous challenges, everyone must work together to find a way off the island before it sinks into the ocean.

A scene from Journey to the Center of the Earth: *Hutcherson (Sean) with Brendan Fraser (Trevor) and Anita Briem (Hannah).*

Cirque du Freak: The Vampire's Assistant

Hutcherson appeared in the 2009 movie *Cirque du Freak: The Vampire's Assistant.* The movie is based on three books in the series *The Saga of Darren Shan,* a comic-goth series for young adults written by Darren Shan. The story focuses on two teenaged best friends, Darren (played by Chris Massoglia) and Steve (played by Hutcherson). Darren is popular and gets good grades in school, while Steve is a troublemaker who is accused of being a bad influence on Darren. When the two friends decide to visit a travelling circus freak show, their lives are changed forever. Darren and Steve are drawn into a long-running conflict between two rival groups, the Vampires and the Vampaneze. Through a dramatic sequence of events, Darren becomes a Vampire and must begin training as a vampire's assistant. Steve soon becomes a Vampaneze, one of the evil clan fighting against the Vampires. The two must then leave their old lives behind and join the travelling band of freaks. Tension rises as the two former friends, now on opposite sides of an ancient rivalry, must determine whether they are destined to become sworn enemies.

The movie received mixed reviews, with critics finding some elements to praise even when dismissing it overall. As Betsy Sharkey wrote in the *Los Angeles Times,* "The themes in *Cirque* are typical teenage ones—feeling like a freak, unsure of who you are or what you want to be in life, ready to fall in love, kinda, especially when the monkey girl (Jessica Carlson) is so cute, and falling out with your best friend…. So it's a disappointment that *Cirque* isn't better. The look of the film has a great, eerie Victorian story-book quality to it. The story and characters are mostly sized for the 8- to 10-year-old crowd. The action—a lot of rough vampire-versus-vampaneze (the killer vamps) fighting, which entails limb tearing, head butting, and spilled blood—aims a little older. Meanwhile the dialogue is shooting for something akin to the campy cleverness of *Scream*. Unfortunately [director Paul Weitz] can't quite get a handle on what the film should be…. *Cirque* is a harmless bit of fluff with a very cool look, but there's just never enough bite." Hutcherson came in for some praise for his performance as Steve, in-cluding these comments from Sandie Angulo Chen on the website Com-mon Sense Media. "Hutcherson, who was brilliant in *Bridge to Terabithia*, nails the insecure, impetuous character of Steve and deserves more lead-ing—not sidekick—roles."

The Kids Are All Right

Hutcherson's next project was the 2010 Academy Award nominated drama *The Kids Are All Right*. He played 15-year-old Laser, who is teetering on the brink of juvenile delinquency, in an all-star cast that included An-nette Bening and Julianne Moore, playing his same-sex parents; Mark Ruf-falo, playing his sperm-donor father; and Mia Wasikoska, playing his sister Joni. When Joni decides that Laser needs a father figure, she tries to track down their father, an anonymous sperm donor. When he shows up to meet the family, everyone must adjust to the new presence in their lives. As the awkward new relationships develop, the kids, the two mothers, and the father all struggle to fit their lives together in a new way.

Hutcherson's portrayal of Laser brought him to the attention of a larger audience of moviegoers and was seen as a big step in advancing his career. "It's not a movie aimed at a particularly teen audience, and I guess that means an 'acting' breakthrough. I hope so," he remarked. "I just know that I was floored—blown away—when I learned who was going to be in it. I mean, these are heavy hitters. I had to be on my toes this time out." *The Kids Are All Right* was widely praised by critics. *USA Today* film reviewer Claudia Puig noted, "The kids come off wiser and more mature in many ways than the adults responsible for them in the warmly funny and intelli-gent *The Kids Are All Right*."

The Hunger Games

Hutcherson next landed the coveted role of Peeta Mellark in the highly an-ticipated 2012 movie *The Hunger Games*. Based on the first book in the wild-ly popular three-book series by Suzanne Collins, *The Hunger Games* is set in

Peeta (Hutcherson) in the Capitol with Cinna (Lenny Kravitz, left) and Haymitch Abernathy (Woody Harrelson, center), before the Games.

the brutal world of Panem, a nation that evolved from the remains of North America after a terrible calamity. Most of the citizens of Panem's 12 districts are forced to work to support the wealthy, tyrannical rulers of the Capitol.

Some time in the past, the people in the districts had gone to war against the Capitol but suffered a terrible defeat. As part of their surrender, each district was forced to agree to send one boy and one girl to participate in "The Hunger Games," an annual televised competition. The 24 competitors, known as "tributes," are selected by lottery. They are taken to the Capitol and locked in an arena where they must fight and kill one another until only one is left alive. The winner is awarded riches and freedom. Peeta, the gentle and kind son of his district's baker, becomes a tribute along with Katniss (played by Jennifer Lawrence), an expert hunter and archer. Peeta and Katniss both must fight in the Games, and there can be only one survivor. The movie also featured Liam Hemsworth as Gale, Woody Harrelson as Haymitch Abernathy, Elizabeth Banks as Effie, Lenny Kravitz as Cinna, and Donald Sutherland as President Snow. (For more information on Suzanne Collins, see *Biography Today,* September 2011; for more information on Jennifer Lawrence, see *Biography Today,* April 2012.)

When Hutcherson learned that *The Hunger Games* would be made into a movie, he knew immediately that he wanted the role of Peeta. "I read the

Hutcherson as Peeta competing during the Games.

whole series in five days. Bam! Bam! Yes, more! Gimme, gimme! Come on!"Hutcherson said, "I don't want to be that actor who's like, 'Yeah, man, the role is so me.' But it is! I am Peeta. His humility, his self-deprecating humor, his way that he can just talk to anybody in any room."Hutcherson was even more confident once filming began. "I've never connected with a character more in my life and felt like I had to act less. It was kind of weird. Like, 'Suzanne Collins, how did you know me? How do you know what I stand for? This is crazy!'"

The Hunger Games was an instant hit with moviegoers and critics alike. Fans flocked to theaters, making *The Hunger Games* the highest earning movie for several weeks after its premiere. *New York Daily News* movie reviewer Joe Neumaier said, "*The Hunger Games*, the highly anticipated movie based on the best-selling teen novel, is as tough-spirited as fans would hope for— and exciting and thought-provoking in a way few adventure dramas ever are.… It's also a far more serious movie than the marketing, and mainstream mania, have led us to believe. It's better and scarier than its source book, and aims an angry eye at our bloodthirsty, watch-anything-and-cheer culture." According to *Rolling Stone* movie reviewer Peter Travers, "Relax, you legions of Hunger Gamers. We have a winner. Hollywood didn't screw up the film version of Suzanne Collins' young-adult bestseller about a survival-of-the-fittest reality show that sends home all its teen contestants, save the victor, in body bags. The screen *Hunger Games* radiates a hot, jumpy energy that's irresistible. It has epic spectacle, yearning romance, suspense that won't quit.… *The Hunger Games* is a zeitgeist movie that captures the spirit of a soul-sucking age in which ego easily trumps common cause." Travers also praised Hutcherson for bringing "humor and a bruised heart to a boy who needs to mature fast."

As one of the stars of the incredibly popular movie, Hutcherson has had to learn to live with fame. So far, he has remained philosophical about all of the extra attention. "I know it's going to be a big change, but I think if you go about it in the right way, you can still have your privacy. You got to just keep on trucking and make sure you're always being true to yourself. Which is so funny be-

"I am Peeta. His humility, his self-deprecating humor, his way that he can just talk to anybody in any room," Hutcherson said. *"I've never connected with a character more in my life and felt like I had to act less. It was kind of weird. Like, 'Suzanne Collins, how did you know me? How do you know what I stand for? This is crazy!'"*

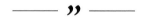

cause—God bless America!—that's exactly what Peeta would say." His performance as Peeta earned him four MTV Movie Award nominations in 2012, including Best Male Performance, Best Cast (shared with *The Hunger Games* costars), Best Fight (shared with Jennifer Lawrence), and Best Kiss (shared with Jennifer Lawrence). Hutcherson has already signed on to play Peeta in *Catching Fire*, the second *Hunger Games* movie.

In 2012, Hutcherson received a Vanguard Award from the Gay and Lesbian Alliance against Defamation (GLAAD). This award recognizes a member of the entertainment industry who has made a significant difference in promoting equal rights for lesbian, gay, bisexual, and transgender people. He is the youngest person to receive the award. Hutcherson was honored for the video he created as part of the Straight But Not Narrow campaign, an educational project that works to reduce homophobia among young heterosexual males.

Future Plans

Hutcherson's next movie role will be in *Red Dawn*, a remake of the 1984 action movie of the same title. The story of a group of teenagers who come together to fight against an invading foreign army as the U.S. stands at the brink of World War III, *Red Dawn* is scheduled to be released in 2012.

Hutcherson plans to continue acting and to become a director someday. "I just sort of followed my passion, and anything I got turned down for, I just kept my head up looking for the next project," he said. "Since I first started, my goal has been to act forever. I knew the transition from child actor into adult actor is one that not everyone gets the luxury of making and some fizzle out. It's about finding the right scripts, doing things that are different."

HOME AND FAMILY

Hutcherson currently lives in California.

SELECTED CREDITS

Kicking & Screaming, 2005
Little Manhattan, 2005
Zathura, 2005
Bridge to Terabithia, 2007
Journey to the Center of the Earth, 2008
Cirque du Freak: The Vampire's Assistant, 2009
The Kids Are All Right, 2010
Journey 2: Mysterious Island, 2012
The Hunger Games, 2012

HONORS AND AWARDS

Leading Young Actor Award (Young Artist Awards): 2006, for *Zathura*; 2008, for *Bridge to Terabithia*
Vanguard Award (Gay and Lesbian Alliance against Defamation— GLAAD): 2012
MTV Movie Awards: 2012 (two awards), Best Male Performance, Best Fight in a Movie (with Jennifer Lawrence and Alexander Ludwig)

FURTHER READING

Periodicals

Current Events, Feb. 12, 2007, p.6
Entertainment Weekly, July 23, 2010, p.67; Aug. 5, 2011, p.44
Girls' Life, Oct./Nov. 2009, p.55
Seventeen, Oct. 2011, p.89
USA Today, Nov. 2, 2005, p.D3

Online Articles

www.allmovie.com/artist/josh-hutcherson-p380181
(AllMovie.com, "Josh Hutcherson," 2012)

www.kidzworld.com/article/25889-josh-hutcherson-bio
  (Kidz World, "Josh Hutcherson Bio," no date)
movies.yahoo.com/person/josh-hutcherson
  (Yahoo, "Josh Hutcherson," no date)

ADDRESS

Josh Hutcherson
ICM Partners
10250 Constellation Boulevard
Los Angeles, CA 90067

WEB SITES

joshhutcherson.com
www.thehungergamesmovie.com
www.suzannecollinsbooks.com
www.scholastic.com/thehungergames

Jerry Mitchell 1959-

American Investigative Reporter
Investigator of Famous Murder Cases from the Civil
Rights Era

BIRTH

Jerry Mitchell Jr. was born in Springfield, Missouri, in 1959.
He was the only child of Jane and Jerry Sr., who served in the
U.S. military as a Navy pilot. Young Jerry, who was nicknamed "Boo" by his parents, spent his earliest years of childhood living on naval bases in California. When his father retired in the mid-1960s, though, the Mitchell family settled in
Texarkana, Texas.

YOUTH

Jerry grew up in a family haunted by illness. He and his parents seemed perfectly healthy, but many members of his father's side of the family suffered from a deadly illness that was so rare that it did not even have a name. Jerry later described the disease as "a monster that [had] lived with my family for more than a century, a monster that first attacks the muscles and then ravages the brain and sometimes bones, a monster that leaves his victims in crumpled heaps, eyes swirling, unable to focus." Symptoms of the disease, which usually appeared before victims reached the age of 50, included severe muscular dystrophy and dementia. The mysterious disease eventually claimed the lives of Jerry's paternal grandfather and all four of his siblings. As Jerry was growing up, his family always lived with the unspoken fear that he or his father might start showing signs of the horrible disease. Their fears were not relieved until the early 2000s, when Jerry and his father participated in a medical research project that revealed that neither man carried the gene responsible for the disease.

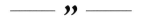

> *Mitchell grew up in the South during an era of great social turmoil. But the civil rights movement did not really make much of an impression on him. "It's like it took place all around me, but in an alternate universe," he later said.*

In most other respects, Jerry experienced the normal childhood of a white kid growing up in the American South in the 1960s. His family was heavily involved in church, he got good grades, and his father gave him basic instruction in sports. Jerry Sr. was a pretty stern and hardnosed coach, though. "Dad never let me win at anything," Jerry recalled. "I'll never forget the day I finally beat him in basketball."

Mitchell grew up during an era of tremendous change in the American South. For centuries, southern whites had used segregation (the separation of schools, restaurants, and other facilities by race), to keep African Americans poor, uneducated, and politically powerless. Many white people felt a deep and abiding prejudice against black people. African-Americans were often treated as inferior, and they were expected to act subservient. The South had been segregated under what were called "Jim Crow" laws. These discriminatory laws forced the segregation of the races and created "separate but equal" public facilities—housing, schools, transportation, bathrooms, drinking fountains, and more—for blacks and

Scenes from the Jim Crow era: a boy using a segregated water fountain (top) and a Ku Klux Klan night rally with Klansmen burning a wooden cross (bottom).

111

whites. Although these separate facilities were called equal, in reality those for blacks were miserably inadequate. African Americans usually attended dilapidated, impoverished schools with underpaid teachers. After leaving school, their opportunities for work were often just as limited.

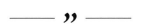

"I'm motivated by the fact that people got away with murder," Mitchell said. "And what makes these crimes more egregious is everybody knew they were getting away with it. It was murder with impunity."

Many African-American people resented the unequal system in which they lived. But the black communities of the American South felt powerless to change things. White men occupied nearly every important political and law enforcement office across the South, and most of them did not want African Americans to gain greater political, economic, or social power. As a result, they used a variety of means to keep black families "in their place." For example, some officials forced African Americans to pass extremely difficult written tests before they would allow them to register to vote. The poll tax—a tax that a person must pay before being permitted to vote—was another popular tool to repress the black vote, because most black people were so poor that they could not afford the expense. Finally, whites used violence and intimidation to make sure that African Americans remained in their inferior position in society.

That began to change during the civil rights era, which flowered across the South during the 1950s and 1960s. During this pivotal period in American history, legendary African-American figures like Martin Luther King Jr., Rosa Parks, John Lewis, and Medgar Evers led activists in a long, difficult, and sometimes deadly struggle for equal civil rights in the United States. This battle was most intense in the South.

The civil rights era generated sickening levels of violence in some parts of the South. Many whites of that period held deeply racist views toward blacks, and they felt free to openly express those feelings at school, church, and places of work. Some whites banded together in white supremacist organizations like the Ku Klux Klan. These groups used violence and intimidation while committing crimes of arson, assault, and murder in an effort to stop the African-American quest for equality. The civil rights movement, though, would not be denied. Thousands of brave African-American demonstrators—aided in some instances by sympathetic white college students and religious leaders from the North—refused to give up. The men and women in the movement persevered in the face of appalling discrimination and violence, and ultimately they were victorious. By the mid-1960s the civil rights movement had spurred the United States to pass a series of laws that outlawed segregation, bestowed equal rights on blacks, guaranteed voting rights, and brought the Jim Crow South crashing down.

Mitchell grew up in the South during this era of great social turmoil. But the civil rights movement did not really make much of an impression on him. "It's like it took place all around me, but in an alternate universe," he later said. Still, his parents made it clear to him that racist talk and attitudes would not be tolerated in their house. "I remember I came home, I was about eight or nine years old, and I said the N-word," Mitchell said. "I learned it from a friend. [My mom] treated me as if it were a capital offense. And I thank God for that. Because she taught me, and my father taught me, about race, and the right ways to treat one another."

EDUCATION

Mitchell earned a bachelor's degree in speech and journalism from Harding University in Searcy, Arkansas, in 1982. He then became a newspaper reporter, but he continued to take classes to further his education. This hard work paid off in 1997, when he received a master's degree in journalism from Ohio State University.

CAREER HIGHLIGHTS

After graduating from college, Mitchell moved to Los Angeles, California, to seek a career as a movie screenwriter. He found little success, though, so he returned to the Southwest in a year or so. Mitchell spent the next few years working for small newspapers in Texas and Arkansas before landing a job in 1986 with the *Jackson (MS) Clarion-Ledger,* a newspaper in Jackson, Mississippi.

Mitchell spent his first few years at the *Clarion-Ledger* working as a general news reporter, but in 1989 he saw a movie that dramatically changed the arc of his career in journalism. He was assigned to cover the opening of the film *Mississippi Burning,* which was loosely based on a Federal Bureau of Investigation (FBI) investigation of a famous civil rights case: a real-life triple murder that had taken place in Mississippi back in 1964. The victims were three civil rights workers named James Chaney, Andrew Goodman, and Michael Schwerner. They had come to Mississippi as part of Freedom Summer, a massive effort by thousands of civil rights activists to register black voters in the South. After their murders, the state of Mississippi refused to file any charges against the suspects. Then the U.S. government stepped in. Federal authorities ultimately convicted seven Ku Klux Klan members of involvement in the murders, but none of them served more than six years in prison. Other key suspects, including alleged ringleader Edgar Ray Killen, went free. Mississippi's legal system was so dominated by whites that investigators were unable to obtain convictions for these crimes. This type of collusion by law enforcement was not uncommon during this period.

Mississippi Burning was criticized in some quarters for being historically inaccurate and failing to acknowledge the bravery of civil rights activists. Nonetheless, the suspenseful film made a huge impression on Mitchell. "I was totally ignorant and stupid of the civil rights movement," he explained. "I always say [the film] was the beginning of my education." Mitchell actually saw the movie with two FBI agents who had been involved on the case. "After the film was over, I wondered aloud why none of these Klansmen had ever been tried for murder," he recalled. "The agents said everyone knew who the killers were, but the state balked at prosecuting, believing convictions were impossible. The agents assured me that these killers were hardly the only ones who had escaped justice in those days."

Reopening Cold Cases of the Civil Rights Era

Mitchell was so inspired by the movie—and so angered by the thought that racist murderers from the civil rights era were still strolling around Mississippi—that he decided to start investigating the state's unsolved murder cases from that period. He did not care that these were "cold cases"—investigations that been closed for years. Mitchell wanted to see these killers brought to justice, and he was prepared to spend a lot of his time and energy trying to uncover evidence that had been missed or covered up by white officials back in the 1960s.

Mitchell decided to start his investigation by examining the secret records of the Mississippi Sovereignty Commission. During the 1960s the agency, which was headed by the governor himself, had been at the forefront of white efforts to stop the civil rights movement. The commission, explained Mitchell, "was a really amazing sort of state-run FBI. Individual states are not supposed to have FBIs in this country, but Mississippi had one, and it was a force for maintaining segregation and otherwise spreading lawlessness, terror, and harassment throughout the state."

Mitchell requested access to the commission's records, but was flatly turned down. These rejections, though, just made him more determined. "When someone tells me I can't have something, I want it a million times worse, right?" he said. "I was told I couldn't have these Sovereignty Com-

MISSING <small>CALL FBI</small>

THE FBI IS SEEKING INFORMATION CONCERNING THE DISAPPEARANCE AT PHILADELPHIA, MISSISSIPPI, OF THESE THREE INDIVIDUALS ON JUNE 21, 1964. EXTENSIVE INVESTIGATION IS BEING CONDUCTED TO LOCATE GOODMAN, CHANEY, AND SCHWERNER, WHO ARE DESCRIBED AS FOLLOWS:

ANDREW GOODMAN **JAMES EARL CHANEY** **MICHAEL HENRY SCHWERNER**

RACE:	White	Negro	White
SEX:	Male	Male	Male
DOB:	November 23, 1943	May 30, 1943	November 6, 1939
POB:	New York City	Meridian, Mississippi	New York City
AGE:	20 years	21 years	24 years
HEIGHT:	5'10"	5'7"	5'9" to 5'10"
WEIGHT:	150 pounds	135 to 140 pounds	170 to 180 pounds
HAIR:	Dark brown; wavy	Black	Brown
EYES:	Brown	Brown	Light blue
TEETH:		Good: none missing	
SCARS AND MARKS:		1 inch cut scar 2 inches above left ear.	Pock mark center of forehead, slight scar on bridge of nose, appendectomy scar, broken leg scar.

SHOULD YOU HAVE OR IN THE FUTURE RECEIVE ANY INFORMATION CONCERNING THE WHEREABOUTS OF THESE INDIVIDUALS, YOU ARE REQUESTED TO NOTIFY ME OR THE NEAREST OFFICE OF THE FBI. TELEPHONE NUMBER IS LISTED BELOW.

DIRECTOR
FEDERAL BUREAU OF INVESTIGATION
UNITED STATES DEPARTMENT OF JUSTICE
WASHINGTON, D. C. 20535
TELEPHONE, NATIONAL 8-7117

June 29, 1964

An FBI missing persons poster showing three civil rights workers, Andrew Goodman, James Earl Chaney, and Michael Henry Schwerner, who were murdered by the Ku Klux Klan. Their case was the basis for the movie Mississippi Burning, *which inspired Mitchell to begin investigating civil rights cases.*

A photo of civil rights worker Medgar Evers in Jackson, Mississippi, about 1960.

mission records, and so I began to develop sources which began to leak me these documents."

As Mitchell examined the secret records, he made a startling discovery about one of the most notorious murders ever to take place in Mississippi. On June 12, 1963, the African-American civil rights activist Medgar Evers had been gunned down in his driveway in Jackson. Evers had been active in a variety of civil rights campaigns; at the time of his death, he was a field officer in Mississippi for the National Association for the Advancement of Colored People (NAACP). Nine days after his murder, Byron De La Beck-with, a white fertilizer salesman with known ties to white supremacist groups, was arrested and charged with his murder. De La Beckwith was put on trial twice, but on both occasions he went free because the jurors could not agree on a verdict. These "hung juries," as they were known, came about despite the fact that the prosecution built a strong case against the accused. Court observers blamed the hung juries on the existence of Jim Crow laws that kept blacks out of the jury box. All of the jurors in both trials were white males.

Achieving Justice for Medgar Evers

Mitchell uncovered evidence in the Sovereignty Commission records that the agency had secretly helped De La Beckwith's defense team during his second trial. It had done so by using taxpayer dollars to investigate potential jurors and help De La Beckwith's lawyers pick jurors who would be supportive of their client.

Armed with this knowledge, Mitchell visited De La Beckwith and his wife, Thelma, at their rural home in Signal Mountain, Tennessee. The journalist spent several hours with the couple, during which time De La Beckwith made vicious and hateful statements about blacks and the white "traitors" who had supported their civil rights activism. The elderly racist also hinted—with great pride and satisfaction—that he was Evers's murderer. "I could feel the evil in them," Mitchell said years later when recalling that visit.

A short time later, Mitchell published a story in the *Clarion-Ledger* detailing his findings about the

Byron De La Beckwith at his home in Mississippi, with a Confederate flag in the background. He was convicted of the murder of Medgar Evers and sent to prison more than 30 years after the crime.

Sovereignty Commission and its role in De La Beckwith's second murder trial. The article prompted Evers's widow, Myrlie Evers Williams, to ask authorities to reopen the case. They did so in October 1989, and over the next several months a new generation of investigators and prosecutors uncovered important new evidence, including the rifle that De La Beckwith had used to assassinate Evers.

In 1993 De La Beckwith was put on trial once again for Evers's murder. This time, however, he was found guilty by a jury of eight blacks and four whites. When the verdict was announced on February 5, 1994, Mitchell felt a tremendous sense of relief and satisfaction. A few days later, though, he received a frightening phone call from the sheriff who had taken De La Beckwith to jail. "[The sheriff] was telling me, 'you know, when we took Beckwith away he kept saying two words,'" remembered Mitchell. "And I was like, 'Really?' He said, 'Yep, two words.' 'What two words?' 'Jerry Mitchell.' So for a minute I'm just kinda like basking in the glow of what I consider this really great compliment and then the sheriff keeps going and says, 'Now when you drive home, Jerry, you know, you might not want to go the same way [you usually do].'"

Mitchell was terrified by the implication that a racist ally of De La Beckwith might try to kill him for his role in the case, but it did not stop him from continuing his investigations. To the contrary, Mitchell has said that his experience with De La Beckwith encouraged him to look into other long-ago crimes against civil rights activists. De La Beckwith spent the last seven years of his life in federal prison before dying in 2001.

Refusing to Buckle Under Pressure

During the mid-1990s Mitchell's journalistic investigations repeatedly dug up new evidence about Mississippi murders related to the civil rights struggles of the 1960s. His efforts sparked a flurry of new police investigations, trials, and convictions for crimes that had gone unpunished for decades.

Mitchell has admitted, though, that these years were full of uncertainty. Although the *Clarion-Ledger* has been supportive of his journalistic efforts for many years, the reporter acknowledged that his early stories triggered strong hostility from some of the paper's executives. "One of the newspaper's top people did oppose my reporting into these brutal unpunished crimes that brought shame to Mississippi's name," he recalled. "I kept expecting to come in one morning and find my computer gone and my cubicle disassembled and me heading back to my hometown, begging for my old job at the *Texarkana Gazette*." Even though a few of his early stories were rejected, though, Mitchell did not despair. "You know what I did? I'm very sneaky," he said. "I just held onto them. So when that editor was gone, I just resurrected the story and ran it…. Just because an editor kills a story, that doesn't mean it's dead for good."

Mitchell also said that his cold-case sleuthing caused grumbling among some Mississippians—and not just racists whose warped views made them sympathetic to people like De La Beckwith. One common complaint was that Mitchell's stories in the *Clarion-Ledger* were making the state look bad. Other critics expressed resentment, as if they were supposed to feel guilty about things that happened in a bygone era. "Many Southerners—including those who never raised a hand to harm anyone else—would rather move forward in a diverse New South than backtrack to the bad old days of Jim Crow, blatant racism, and murder," explained scholar R. Hayes Johnson in *Human Rights.* "A whole generation of Southerners has been born since the peak of the civil rights movement,

Smoke rises from the firebombed home of civil rights leader Vernon Dahmer.

and many of those younger people—especially whites—are quick to note that they had nothing to do with the crimes and misdeeds of the previous generations."

Mitchell does not have much patience with these complaints, though. In his view, the most important thing to remember is that his reporting helps bring murderers to justice. "I'm motivated by the fact that people got away with murder," he said. "And what makes these crimes more egregious is everybody knew they were getting away with it. It was murder with impunity."

Taking Down a Klan Wizard

In early 1998 Mitchell received information from a secret source about another notorious assassination of the civil rights era—the slaying of Vernon Dahmer in a firebombing of his house in Hattiesburg, Mississippi, on January 10, 1966. Dahmer was a business leader, a civil rights activist, and the president of the local NAACP chapter who was leading the local voters' registration drives. On the night of the attack, the family was at home when several carloads of white Klansmen burst into the house and set it on fire. Dahmer held them off while his wife and children managed to escape, but he died from his severe burns. Authorities ultimately brought 13 white men to trial for involvement in his murder, but only four of them were convicted, and none of the four served more than ten years in prison. The man who ordered the firebombing was Sam Bowers, who had been the "Imperial Wizard" (supreme leader) of an extremely violent offshoot of the Ku Klux Klan in Mississippi during the 1960s. Bowers was put on trial for Dahmer's murder four times, but the jury deadlocked every time, enabling the Klan leader to walk away a free man.

Mitchell talked to an informant about the case. He learned that Billy Roy Pitts, one of the four Klansmen convicted of the Dahmer murder, had never served a day in prison. Instead, Mississippi authorities had let him go, telling everyone that he was in a witness protection program. The journalist quickly tracked Pitts down in Louisiana. Pitts was horrified when Mitchell confronted him. Eager to avoid prison and wracked with guilt over his role in Dahmer's murder, Pitts agreed to testify against Bowers. When prosecutors re-opened the case, they subsequently found other important evidence to use against the Klan leader. Bowers was convicted of murder in 1998, and he spent the last eight years of his life in prison.

The conviction of Bowers gave Dahmer's wife and children a measure of peace that had eluded them ever since his death nearly a half-century ago. "Once this settles in and I get control of my emotions,"Vernon Dahmer Jr. told Mitchell, "I am going to the cemetery and pray and tell my father that justice finally came and he can begin to rest in peace."

Uncovering a Murderer's Fake Alibi

Mitchell also began investigating another infamous event of the civil rights era: the 1963 bombing of a black church in Birmingham, Alabama, that killed four young girls. The four girls—Denise McNair, age 11, and Addie Mae Collins, Carole Robertson, and Cynthia Wesley, all age 14— were in the basement of the 16th Street Baptist Church talking about the start of school and getting ready for services when the bomb exploded. Investigators had identified four members of a Ku Klux Klan group as the prime suspects, but they were unable to secure convictions against any of them during the 1960s. In 1977 the case was re-opened, and one of the Klansmen was convicted and sent to prison. Another one died in 1994 as a free man. For many years it appeared that the other two suspects, white supremacists Bobby Frank Cherry and Thomas Blanton Jr., would also avoid prison. In the late 1990s, though, authorities in Alabama opened the case once again.

Blanton and Cherry both maintained their longstanding claims that they were innocent. Cherry even decided to call Mitchell, who by this time had become one of the best-known journalists in the South, to proclaim his innocence. Mitchell promptly accepted Cherry's offer to come to his home for a chat, and a few days later he spent about six hours visiting with Cherry and his wife. During their conversation Cherry repeated his long-time claim that he was home watching wrestling on television at the time of the crime. When he returned to his office, Mitchell decided to check Cherry's alibi. He instructed an assistant to check and make sure that a wrestling program had in fact been broadcast on television the day of the bombing. As it turned out, though, none of the stations had carried wrestling that day.

Mitchell's discovery opened the floodgates for investigators. As Cherry's alibi fell apart, they found new evidence that enabled them to make stronger cases against

Sam Bowers is helped up the courthouse steps by Deputy Ronald Taylor on his way to court on charges of murder and arson against Vernon Dahmer.

both of the old Klansmen. "For three and a half decades [Cherry's] alibi had basically gone unchallenged, and now, lo and behold his alibi doesn't stand up," said the reporter. "There hadn't been wrestling on [television] for years. And it's always struck me as so stupid. It seems to me if you're a criminal, and you've got your to-do list, it seems like the first thing, number one on the list, would be 'One: Check alibi.' Eh, we're not dealing with people with really high IQs."

In the end, both Cherry and Blanton were convicted of four counts of murder in the 1963 Birmingham church bombing. Blanton's conviction came on May 1, 2001, and he remained in prison as of 2012. Cherry received a life sentence on May 22, 2001. He died in prison in November 2004.

Returning to the *Mississippi Burning* Case

At the same time that Mitchell was helping bring the Birmingham church bombers to justice after nearly 40 years, he also undertook a separate investigation into the 1964 murders that had been featured in the movie *Mississippi Burning*. These were the killings of three civil rights workers—James Chaney, Andrew Goodman, and Michael Schwerner—that had first inspired him to dedicate his career to murder cases of the civil rights era.

Mitchell's involvement in the case occurred by chance. During the course of his investigation into the Vernon Dahmer murder, he had learned a secret about Sam Bowers, the Klan Imperial Wizard who had ordered the firebombing of the Dahmer home. In 1983 Bowers had given a secret interview to the Mississippi state archivist, an official responsible for keeping historical records for the state. Bowers had agreed to the interview under the condition that it be sealed from the public until his death. In 1998, however, Mitchell got his hands on a transcript of the interview.

Mitchell has been successful because he refused to let death threats or other forms of intimidation get in his way. "I don't live in fear," he said. "I think it's one of those bridges I had to cross early as a reporter. Am I going to keep reporting on this or not, you know? Just because I get threats, am I going to stop? You know, I decided no. And it does go back to my faith, you know, on a personal level and I've been able to persist at this and thankfully some of these [murderers] have been prosecuted and gone behind bars."

Mitchell was stunned by what he read. During the course of the interview Bowers denied direct involvement in the June 1964 killings of Chaney, Goodman, and Schwerner. The Klan leader added, however, that he organized a campaign of lies to keep the murder investigators from the true mastermind, a Baptist preacher named Edgar Ray Killen. Bowers's scheme worked. Killen was charged with murder in the three killings, but he was acquitted of all charges in 1967. As a result, "I was quite delighted to be convicted and have the main instigator of the entire affair walk out of the courtroom a free man," Bowers said with satisfaction. "Everybody—including the trial judge and the prosecutors and everybody else—knows that that happened."

The burned shell of the station wagon used by the three murdered civil rights workers was found in a swampy area near Philadelphia, Mississippi, 1964. Their killer, Edgar Ray Killen, shown here in court, was convicted after more than 40 years.

123

Mitchell promptly wrote an article in the *Clarion-Ledger* that exposed Bowers's statements. The paper also published excerpts from the interview detailing Killen's orders to kill the three young activists. This bombshell story convinced state authorities to put Killen on trial again. In 2005 Killen was convicted of three counts of manslaughter and sentenced to three 20-year prison terms. These sentences ensured that the white supremacist would spend the rest of his life behind bars.

Solving Puzzles

Mitchell believes that one of the keys to his journalistic success over the years is that he seems so familiar to the men and women he interviews. "I think they talk to me because I am like them, a white Southerner, raised a Christian," he explained. "Being a Southerner is what enabled me to do these stories. If I'd not had a Southern accent, these Klan guys wouldn't have talked to me. Being willing to go out for barbecue and catfish helped, too."

—— **"** ——

Mitchell believes that one of the keys to his journalistic success is that he seems so familiar to the men and women he interviews. "I think they talk to me because I am like them, a white Southerner, raised a Christian," he explained. "Being a Southerner is what enabled me to do these stories. If I'd not had a Southern accent, these Klan guys wouldn't have talked to me. Being willing to go out for barbecue and catfish helped, too."

—— **"** ——

Another key for Mitchell is that he enjoys the intellectual challenge of finding evidence that will enable authorities to convict killers of yesteryear. "It's like putting a puzzle together," he said. "Sometimes you have pieces and you don't know how they match up. And then years later, you get some more information and suddenly it all makes sense and it all fits together.... I very much work like a detective almost, in terms of trying to piece the case together."

Finally, Mitchell has been successful because he refused to let death threats or other forms of intimidation get in his way. "I don't live in fear," he said. "I think it's one of those bridges I had to cross early as a reporter. Am I going to keep reporting on this or not, you know? Just because I get threats, am I going to stop? You know, I decided no. And it does go back to my faith, you know, on a personal level and I've been able to persist at

Mitchell at his desk in the Clarion-Ledger *newsroom.*

this and thankfully some of these [murderers] have been prosecuted and gone behind bars."

Mitchell also notes that he receives more support from the public than he once did. "When I first started writing about this there were a lot of unhappy people," he admitted. "But as time went on, as there were arrests and there were convictions and those kinds of things, attitudes began to kinda change.... You know, in 1964, there were hardly any African Americans registered to vote in Mississippi. Today in Mississippi there are more [African-American] elected officials than any other state. So you can see, Mississippi has really come a long way. That's not to say it doesn't still have a long ways to go, but it's certainly come a long way."

Becoming One of America's Most Respected Reporters

Mitchell's success in solving cold cases of the civil rights era has inspired many southern states to re-open unsolved murder cases from those years. As of 2011, those investigations have led to a total of 23 convictions for murder and other crimes against civil rights activists and others.

In addition, Mitchell's work has made him one of the nation's most respected journalists. He has received more than 30 national journalism awards, and in 2005 he became the youngest recipient of Columbia University's prestigious John Chancellor Award for Excellence in Journalism. "Mitchell pursued these stories after most people believed they belonged to history, and not to journalism," said famed journalist David Halberstam, who presented the award to Mitchell. "But they did belong to journalism, because the truth had never been told and justice had never been done." Halberstam went on to describe Mitchell as "the most distinguished reporter in the entire country" and "a reflection of what one reporter with a conscience can do."

Mitchell's employers at the *Clarion-Ledger* echo these sentiments. "I just can't say enough about what Jerry has done for journalism and for the history of Mississippi," said *Clarion-Ledger* executive editor Ronnie Agnew in 2007. In recognition of their star reporter's high profile, the newspaper even gave Mitchell his own blog on its website, called "Journey to Justice."

MARRIAGE AND FAMILY

Mitchell lives in Mississippi with his wife and two children.

HOBBIES AND OTHER INTERESTS

Mitchell enjoys working on jigsaw puzzles and listening to music, but he says that he spends most of his free time on writing projects. In 1998 he published a 13-part series in the *Clarion-Ledger* called "The Preacher and the Klansman," which tells the true story of how a preacher and civil rights activist became friends with a former Klansman in Mississippi. Six years later, the newspaper published "Genetic Disaster," a 10-part series in which Mitchell described his family's battle against the rare genetic disease that claimed his grandfather's life. He also continued to write screenplays with an old childhood friend. In 2012 Mitchell announced that he was taking a temporary leave of absence from the *Clarion-Ledger* to complete a book about his work on some of the most notorious murders from the civil rights era.

SELECTED WRITINGS

"The Preacher and the Klansman," 1998
"Genetic Disaster," 2004

SELECTED HONORS AND AWARDS

Outstanding Achievement by an Individual Award (Gannett Newspapers): 1999, 2006
Best Investigative Reporting Award (Gannett Newspapers): 1999
William Ringle Outstanding Achievement Career Award (Gannett Newspapers): 1999
Chancellor Award for Excellence in Journalism (Columbia University): 2005

George Polk Award for Justice Reporting (Long Island University): 2005
Pulitzer Prize for Journalism finalist: 2006
Tom Renner Award for Crime Reporting (Investigative Reporters and Editors): 2006
MacArthur Fellowship (John D. and Catherine T. MacArthur Foundation): 2009
Ralph McGill Medal for Journalistic Courage (University of Georgia): 2009

FURTHER READING

Periodicals

American Journalism Review, Apr.-May 2005
Atlanta Journal-Constitution, June 26, 2005, p.A12
Editor & Publisher, Oct. 30, 2009
Human Rights, Fall 2000, p.18
Jackson (MS) Clarion-Ledger, Aug. 22, 1998
Mother Jones, Jan. 24, 2007
Newsweek, July 4, 2005, p.36
Nieman Reports, Fall 2011, p.17
USA Today, Jan. 17, 2005, p.A4; June 22, 2005, p.A1
USA Today Magazine, July 2011, p.28
Washington Post, Aug. 23, 2009

Online Articles

www.clarionledger.com/apps/pbcs.dll/article?AID=/99999999/special17/60416008
(Clarion Ledger, "Jerry Mitchell's Entry and Biography,"Oct. 22, 2009)
www.journalism.columbia.edu/page/432-2005-chancellor-award-winner-jerry-mitchell/185
(Columbia Journalism School, "2005 Chancellor Award Winner: Jerry Mitchell,"2005)
www.npr.org/templates/story/story.php?storyId=7399590
(National Public Radio, "Reporter Jerry Mitchell on Civil Rights-Era Cold Cases,"Feb. 14, 2007)
www.pbs.org.newshour/media/clarion/mitchell.html
(PBS Online NewsHour, "Jerry Mitchell,"Apr. 18, 2002)
www.pbs.org/newshour/media/clarion/kc_summer.html
(PBS Online NewsHour, "Pursuing the Past: A Mississippi Newspaper Investigates Crimes of the Civil Rights Era,"June 27, 2005)
civilrightsandthepress.syr.edu/index.html
(S.I. Newhouse School of Public Communications, Syracuse University, "Hodding Carter Lecture on Civil Rights and the Press,"no date)

ADDRESS

Jerry Mitchell
The Clarion-Ledger
PO Box 40
Jackson, MS 39205-0040

WEB SITES

blogs.clarionledger.com/jmitchell/about/
blogs.clarionledger.com/jmitchell/
www.coldcases.org
civilrights.historybeat.com/gn_civilrights_investigations.php

Chloë Grace Moretz 1997

American Film Actress
Star of the Movies *Diary of a Wimpy Kid, Hugo,* and
Dark Shadows

BIRTH

Chloë Grace Moretz was born on February 10, 1997, in Atlanta, Georgia. Her father, McCoy "Mac" Moretz, is a plastic
surgeon, and her mother, Teri (Duke) Moretz, is a nurse practi-
tioner. She has four older brothers: Brandon, Trevor, Colin,
and Ethan. Trevor, an actor and producer who performs under
the name Trevor Duke, also serves as Chloë 's acting coach.

YOUTH

Chloë spent her earliest years in Atlanta. She moved to New York City in 2001 with her mother and Trevor when he was accepted at the Professional Performing Arts High School. She became interested in acting while helping him learn his lines. "When Trevor was 15 and I was five, he'd be practicing his monologues, and I just started memorizing them too," she remarked. "I guess something clicked." Soon she began modeling in national print ads and commercials.

In 2003 her family moved to Los Angeles for her father's medical practice. Chloë continued modeling and at age seven landed her first professional acting job as Violet in two episodes of the television drama "The Guardian." Shortly thereafter she started working in film, landing the role of Molly in the 2005 independent drama *Heart of the Beholder*. Her big break came when she was cast in the 2005 remake of the supernatural slasher movie *The Amityville Horror.*

EDUCATION

Moretz attended school until third grade, at which point she started a distance-learning program at home. She is home-schooled by a private tutor for six hours a day when she is working on a film and taught by her mother when she is not on set. A self-proclaimed "history geek," Moretz has talked about her admiration for Martha Washington as a historical figure and her fascination with the Victorian era of the 19th century. When she gets to college, she hopes to continue studying history, along with other subjects. "I'm hopefully going to Columbia University," she stated. "I want to do a minor in Art History and major in Criminal Psychology. I find criminal psychology incredibly fascinating and scary ... how volatile the human mind can be. And I really love classical art."

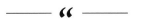

> *Moretz became interested in acting while helping her older brother Trevor, who was studying acting. "When Trevor was 15 and I was five, he'd be practicing his monologues, and I just started memorizing them too," she remarked. "I guess something clicked."*

CAREER HIGHLIGHTS

Becoming an Actress

Moretz launched her film career at the age of eight with the remake of *The Amityville Horror,* which was re-

A scene from The Amityville Horror, *with Moretz (as Chelsea Lutz) in the right window and Isabel Conner (as Jodie Defeo) in the left window.*

leased in 2005. Her character, Chelsea "Missy" Lutz, befriends the ghost of a young girl named Jodie who had been murdered—along with five other family members—in the same Long Island house into which Chelsea's family has recently moved. This horror movie had gory special effects, disturbing subject matter, and an R-rating, so Moretz was not allowed to see it when it was released. However, critics praised her assured, mature performance, saying that with this role she proved that she was capable of handling dark material, even if she was not old enough to watch the movie. Her believability in *The Amityville Horror* led to offers for several other horror projects, including the zombie movie *Wicked Little Things* (2006), in which she played Emma Tunny, and the supernatural thriller *The Eye* (2008), in which she appeared as young cancer patient Alicia Milstone.

From 2007 to 2010, Moretz was heard as the voice of Darby in the Disney Channel's computer-animated TV series "My Friends Tigger & Pooh." Her character is a brave, six-year-old redhead who, along with her dog Buster, befriends the gang from the Hundred Acre Wood. She also voiced the character in several direct-to-DVD Winnie the Pooh movies. In 2008 she played the voice of Young Penny in the celebrated Disney feature *Bolt,* an animated adventure story starring John Travolta and Miley Cyrus about a dog that believes he has superpowers because he has spent his life on the set of a TV series about a superhero canine.

Moretz also continued to perform in live-action pieces, both in movies and on TV. She appeared in the 2006 crime comedy *Big Momma's House 2,* which starred Martin Lawrence as an FBI agent who goes undercover as Big Momma, using this disguise while he's fighting crime. Moretz played Carrie Fuller, part of the family where Big Momma works as a nanny. Despite being panned by critics, the film grossed more than $138 million worldwide. The following year she landed a recurring role as the sweet and talkative Kiki George in the TV drama "Dirty Sexy Money," which ran on ABC from 2007 to 2009. She returned to the silver screen in the 2009 movie *(500) Days of Summer* playing Rachel, the wise-beyond-her-years little sister who offers her lovesick brother sound relationship advice. Critics overwhelmingly praised the romantic comedy as clever, charming, and refreshingly honest. As reviewer Michael Ordoña stated in the *Los Angeles Times,* "*(500) Days of Summer* is something seldom seen: an original romantic comedy. It bristles with energy, emotion, and intellect, as it flits about the dizzying highs and weeping-karaoke lows of a passionate entanglement."

In 2010 Moretz appeared in the comedic film *Diary of a Wimpy Kid,* which is based on the first book in the popular series by Jeff Kinney (for more information on Kinney, see *Biography Today,* January 2011). The *Wimpy Kid* books use humor and cartoon drawings to depict some of the challenges that accompany the transition to middle school. The movie shows the humiliating and intimidating moments in the life of 11-year-old Greg Heffley, both at home and at school. It follows his misadventures with his best friend and sidekick, Rowley Jefferson, as they endure bullies, popularity contests, and gym class, among other trials. Moretz plays Angie Steadman, a student journalist who hangs out under the bleachers reading poetry until she becomes the first girl to notice Greg and Rowley. The movie was a hit with young viewers but received mixed reviews from critics, although many were pleasantly surprised by it. According to Roger Ebert, "It is so hard to do a movie like this well. *Diary of a Wimpy Kid* is a PG-rated comedy about the hero's first year of middle school, and it's nimble, bright, and funny. It doesn't dumb down. It doesn't patronize."

Action and Adventure

Moretz next lit up the silver screen in a leading role as Mindy Macready, also known a Hit-Girl, in the hyper-violent superhero film *Kick-Ass* (2010). She became interested in doing an action film after seeing billboards for the movie *Wanted.* She told her mom, "I really want to do an Angelina Jolie-type character. You know, like an action hero, woman empowerment, awesome, take-charge leading role." A month later they received the script

Moretz as Angie in a scene from Diary of a Wimpy Kid, *with Rowley (Robert Capron, left) and Greg (Zachary Gordon, middle).*

for *Kick-Ass*—the film adaptation of Mark Millar's graphic novel series of the same name. Moretz doesn't usually read movie scripts; instead, her mother reads them first to sort out which are appropriate. This time, her mother knew it was exactly what Chloë wanted. As soon as she found out about the part, Moretz was determined to get the job. "I read it and I freaked out and said, 'I have to be Hit-Girl, mom!' She was like, 'Okay, well—let's try it,'" she recalled. "So I went out to audition for [director Matthew Vaughn], and I got it ... and then I started training!" Moretz trained in martial arts, gymnastics, and weapons handling to play the pre-teen vigilante. "Every single day I would wake up, do crunches, pull-ups, push-ups and go do my training, then come home and go running and swimming,"she remembered. "Somewhere in there, I would fit in school."

The film, and Moretz's role in particular, proved controversial due to the violence and foul language used by Hit-Girl. Moretz was only 11 years old at the time of filming. When asked about the decision to allow Chloë to be part of an adult-oriented production, her mother told the *Sunday Times*, "It definitely pushes boundaries, but Chloë knows the things that Hit-Girl says and does are fictional." She added that she saw it as an opportunity for her to show her grit and athleticism. Moretz has responded to questions about Hit-Girl's use of weapons and obscene language by emphasizing that the character's words and actions are far removed from her own. "If I even uttered a cuss word, I'd be dead. My mom is very strict. It's not real-life. I'm not going around cussing and killing people and pulling out knives. I'm a normal 14-year-old girl," she insisted.

Kick-Ass was popular with audiences, but critics were divided in their reviews. For example, Chris Hewitt of *Empire* magazine hailed it as "a ridiculously entertaining, perfectly paced, ultra-violent cinematic rush," while Roger Ebert panned it as "morally reprehensible." Critics who liked the film praised Moretz's performance, and *Entertainment Weekly* named her among the Top 10 performers to watch in 2010. The director, Matthew Vaughn, echoed the endorsement. In the voiceover commentary to the *Kick-Ass* DVD, Vaughn asserted "You are watching a star being born." Correspondingly, critics have compared Moretz to actresses Jodie Foster and Natalie Portman, both of whom rose to fame in controversial roles when they were about her age.

Following her attention-getting performance in *Kick-Ass,* Moretz was flooded with film offers. She starred in *Let Me In* (2010), a remake of the Swedish vampire film *Let the Right One In,* as a 250-year-old vampire. Critic Mary Pols of *Time* praised her performance, saying "In her latest, *Let Me In,* the 13-year-old gives a transfixing, delicately intuitive performance as Abby, an ancient vampire trapped in the inconvenient shell of a child's body." The movie received positive reviews by most commentators, including *New York Times* reviewer A. O. Scott, who hailed it as "at once artful and unpretentious, more interested in intimacy and implication than in easy scares or slick effects."

Hugo

Moretz next appeared in the 3-D adventure film *Hugo* (2011), based on the novel *The Invention of Hugo Cabret* by Brian Selznick and directed by the acclaimed filmmaker Martin Scorsese. But to get through the audition, she first had to trick the director. "I heard that [Scorsese] was only really looking at British girls. When I went in I was like: 'I'll do whatever I have to do to be in this movie.'" The casting director agreed not to tell Scorsese that she was an American, and when she delivered a spot-on accent in her audition, he mistook her for a native Brit. Three days later she was cast as Isabelle, a bookish girl growing up in Paris in the 1930s. "I went up to the balcony in my house and screamed at the top of my lungs: 'No way! Oh my gosh!'" she recalled.

Hugo is about a French orphan, played by Asa Butterfield, who lives alone in a Paris train station and keeps the railway clocks running. At the same

A scene from Hugo: *Moretz as Isabelle and Asa Butterfield as Hugo, with the mechanical man.*

time, he is trying to repair the mechanical man left by his late father, a watchmaker. With Isabelle's help, Hugo unlocks the secret that his father had left for him, a discovery that changes his life. To help Moretz prepare for her role, Scorsese asked her to study classic Audrey Hepburn films. "It was really what I based Isabelle off of—that fun girl, kinda naïve but sweet and full of wonderment." She has said that of all the characters she has played, she relates most to the fun-loving yet studious Isabelle. "She just loves reading books and those are her adventures," she explained. "Isabelle is a heightened version of my personality."

Hugo was released in 2011 and met with largely positive reviews. *New York Times* critic Manohla Dargis proclaimed, "It's serious, beautiful, wise to the absurdity of life, and in the embrace of a piercing longing." *Entertainment Weekly* critic Lisa Schwarzbaum called the movie "a haunting, piquant melodrama about childhood dreams and yearnings, enhanced with a pleasant survey course in early film history." Likewise, Todd McCarthy of the *Hollywood Reporter* asserted that "Craft and technical achievements are of the highest order, combining to create an immaculate present to film lovers everywhere." He singled out Moretz's performance for particular praise. "Moretz, with her beaming warmth and great smile, is captivating as a girl who leaps at the chance for some adventure outside of books." *Hugo* was nominated for 11 Academy Awards and won five.

———— " ————

"Everyone around me is so strict about keeping me grounded. My mom won't let anyone treat me like a little princess," Moretz claimed. "Honestly, I don't have the room to go crazy, with four brothers and my mom."

———— " ————

Recent Work

In 2012 Moretz was featured in the Tim Burton film *Dark Shadows* starring Johnny Depp and Michelle Pfeiffer. The movie, which was based on a TV soap opera that aired from 1966 to 1971, is about a vampire who awakens after 200 years and joins his dysfunctional descendants in the 1970s. Moretz plays Carolyn Stoddard, an angst-ridden teenager who loves music and fashion but harbors a dark secret. "Carolyn is just like me but a heightened, ruder version of who I am," she explained. "I'm not that mean to my mom and I don't brood nearly as much as she does, but I understand her." Viewers agreed that Depp's performance as Barnabas Collins was the highlight of the movie. Critical response to the movie overall was mixed, with Manohla Dargis of the *New York Times* deeming it "Burton's most pleasurable film in years" and *Los Angeles Times* reviewer Kenneth Turan criticizing its "woeful lack of concern with story and drama."

HOME AND FAMILY

The Moretz family works as a team to prevent Chloë from growing up too quickly and to shield her from the negative influences of Hollywood culture. "Everyone around me is so strict about keeping me grounded. My mom won't let anyone treat me like a little princess," she explained. "Honestly, I don't have the room to go crazy, with four brothers and my mom." Chloë has often commented on her mother's no-nonsense parenting style. For example, her mother confiscated her phone and computer when she spent too much time surfing social networks and playing video games. Her mother has also made a conscious effort not to treat her differently because she is a celebrity. "I still get grounded," she admitted. "They make it very apparent that I'm just a normal girl, and if I ever started behaving like I was anything else I'd be out of the business in a flash."

Her brothers are particularly protective when it comes to the subject of dating. "I had a lot of friends and guys that I think are cute and stuff," she explained, "but it doesn't really work out with the family and all. My family's a bit too big and a bit too abrasive." Still, she recognizes the advantages of being the youngest. "The best thing about having four big brothers is

The cast of Dark Shadows *(from left): Helena Bonham Carter, Chloë Grace Moretz, Eva Green, Gulliver McGrath, Bella Heathcote, Johnny Depp, Ray Shirley, Jackie Earle Haley, Jonny Lee Miller, and Michelle Pfeiffer.*

you always have someone to do something for you," she teased. "No, no. I think number one would be that they always protect me. There's someone to turn to. It's like having four fathers, basically."

Trevor is an especially important influence in Chloë's life. He is not only her brother, but also her acting coach and manager. He often accompanies her on press appearances and travels with her on location. According to Chloë , Trevor helps her develop her characters and bring her performance to the next level. "The way I like to put it is, it's like a painting. I draw the outline, and he fills it in and makes it perfect," she said. Her mom is also involved in her career. "Mom is everything all at once—hair, make-up, mom, everything. It's pretty crazy," she marveled.

When she is not filming, Chloë lives in a house in Los Angeles with her mother. "It's so cute. It's this little place for Mom and me," she said. She also shares her home with an expanding brood of pets, including three dogs—Fuller, Missy, and Bella—and a cat named Zoe.

HOBBIES AND OTHER INTERESTS

Moretz enjoys a variety of activities, including shopping, going to birthday parties, cooking with her mom, and having sleepovers with friends.

She loves to play video games and to interact with friends and fans on Twitter. She also likes traveling and attending music concerts. For exercise, she enjoys ballet, gymnastics, basketball, and swimming. She is a fan of comic-book films, including *Spider-Man* and *The Dark Knight*, but she has admitted to being terrified of scary movies. She has eclectic musical tastes and has listed Lady Gaga, Adele, and Skrillex as a few of her favorite artists.

Moretz and her sense of style have been noticed by the fashion world, and she has recently been featured in a variety of fashion magazines. "I love fashion! To me, it's another way to express myself," she said. She enjoys participating in photo shoots and attending couture fashion shows, but her mother forbids her from wearing high fashion brands when she is not at a movie premiere or red carpet event. For special events she likes the designers Calvin Klein, Chanel, Dior, and Stella McCartney, and for everyday she likes the labels Topshop, American Apparel, and Urban Outfitters.

Moretz is involved with the Starlight Children's Foundation, a charity that helps children cope with chronic and life-threatening illnesses. As a StarPower Ambassador for the organization, she uses her celebrity status to brighten the lives of patients through hospital visits and online chats.

SELECTED CREDITS

Movies

Heart of the Beholder, 2005
The Amityville Horror, 2005
Big Momma's House 2, 2006
Wicked Little Things, 2006
The Eye, 2008
Bolt, 2008
(500) Days of Summer, 2009
Diary of a Wimpy Kid, 2010
Kick-Ass, 2010
Let Me In, 2010
Hugo, 2011
Dark Shadows, 2012

Television

"Dirty Sexy Money," 2007-2008
"My Friends Tigger & Pooh," 2007-2010

HONORS AND AWARDS

Scream Awards (Spike TV): 2010, Best Breakthrough Performance—Female, for *Kick-Ass*; 2011, Best Horror Actress, for *Let Me In*
Empire Awards (*Empire* magazine): 2011, Best Newcomer
MTV Movie Awards: 2011 (two awards), Best Breakout Star and Biggest Badass Star, for *Kick-Ass*
Saturn Awards (The Academy of Science Fiction, Fantasy & Horror Films): 2011, Best Performance by a Younger Actor, for *Let Me In*
Young Artist Awards (Young Artist Foundation): 2011, Best Performance in a Feature Film—Young Ensemble Cast, for *Diary of a Wimpy Kid*
Max Mara Face of the Future Awards (Women in Film) 2012

FURTHER READING

Periodicals

Guardian, Dec. 2, 2011, p.5
Interview, Nov. 2011, p.58
Sunday Times, Oct. 24, 2010, p.12
Teen Vogue, Oct. 2010, p.99; Dec. 2011/Jan. 2012, p.138
Time, Oct. 11, 2010, p.59
Variety, Oct. 22, 2010, p.A9

Online Articles

www.interviewmagazine.com
    (Interview, "Another Hit: Chloë Moretz," Oct. 1, 2010; "Chloë Moretz," Jan. 1, 2012)
www.time.com
    (Time, "Young Blood," Oct. 11, 2010)
whosnews.usaweekend.com
    (USA Weekend, "Meet Chloë Moretz, the Precocious Teen Star of 'Kick-Ass,'" Apr. 9, 2010)
www.variety.com
    (Variety, Youth Impact Report 2010, "Chloë Grace Moretz: Gets a Kick Out of Diverse Roles," Oct. 22, 2010)

ADDRESS

Chloë Grace Moretz
William Morris Endeavor
9601 Wiltshire Blvd. Ste. 3
Beverly Hills, CA 90212

WEB SITE

chloemoretz.com

Francisco Núñez 1965-

American Conductor and Composer
Founder and Artistic Director of the Young People's
Chorus of New York City

BIRTH

Francisco J. Núñez was born in 1965 in New York, New York.
His parents, Emanuel Núñez and Ysmaela Marmolejos, were
both from the Dominican Republic but had emigrated to the
United States before he was born. Francisco is the younger of
their two sons.

YOUTH

Núñez was not very close to his father, who worked as an engineer. Emanuel Núñez wasn't too involved with the family, and he died when Francisco was 14 years old. Marmolejos essentially raised her children as a single parent. Although nobody in her family was formally trained or had made a profession in the arts, they were all very artistic by nature. "My mom always wanted to be a pianist and a ballerina herself," Núñez remembered. "But she had to work, so she left school in seventh grade and worked." In New York, Marmolejos was employed as a seamstress in the garment industry. Although she wasn't able to pursue her dreams of being a professional musician or dancer, she didn't give up her love of music. She bought a beat-up piano at a resale shop, brought it home and began to teach her sons to play.

> *When he took part in music competitions, Núñez met kids from all different ethnic and economic backgrounds who shared a common interest in music. "Classical music has always represented an educated sphere, whether you are poor or rich," he said. "And it taught me that you have to work hard to achieve something."*

Núñez was only five years old at the time, but he took to the piano right away and would experiment with it for hours. His mother was delighted. They lived in the Washington Heights area of New York City, which had a high crime rate. "She was afraid of losing us to the streets," he explained. To give her sons something productive to do rather than just hanging out and getting into trouble, Marmolejos began giving them piano lessons and insisting that they put in long hours of practice. It soon became clear that Núñez had an incredible natural talent for music. When his mother had taught him everything she could about the piano, she found more experienced instructors for him. She and her sons frequently traveled back and forth from New York to the Dominican Republic, and in both places, Núñez had a piano and practiced six or seven hours daily. He focused particularly on works by Latin composers.

As his skill increased, Núñez also entered the world of music recitals and competitions. Those experiences changed his life forever. In New York, a huge variety of ethnic groups coexist, but people often remain within their own neighborhoods, sheltered from cultures other than their own, even when the people live nearby. When he took part in music competitions,

Núñez leading practice for a group of students.

Núñez met kids from all different ethnic and economic backgrounds who shared a common interest in music. "Classical music has always represented an educated sphere, whether you are poor or rich," he said. "And it taught me that you have to work hard to achieve something."

In addition to playing music, Núñez was also learning to compose it. At the age of 15 he composed his first serious choral work, entitled "Misa Pequeña." His hard work wasn't only confined to the world of music, though. Because the family didn't have much money, he got his first job at the age of 11, working on Saturdays at a doughnut shop "to make money and afford stuff other kids had," he remembered.

EDUCATION

Núñez attended public and Catholic schools in both the Dominican Republic and New York City. His mother had been such a strong supporter of his musical endeavors throughout his childhood, but when the time came for college, she strongly urged him to study engineering, which she considered a more practical career choice. Núñez did start out in the engineering program at Manhattan College, but he didn't stay there long. He transferred to New York University, where he earned a bachelor's degree in piano performance in 1988. He later earned a degree in music education from the University of Calgary.

EARLY CAREER

Bringing Music to the Children's Aid Society

According to Núñez, music has enriched his life and brought him into contact with people and situations he would never have encountered without it. After graduating from college, he wanted to do something for society that would help other children from poor economic backgrounds to benefit from music, as he had. "I wanted to take kids from neighborhoods where you couldn't play in the street, combine them with kids from other groups, and use music to instill a sense of discipline," he declared.

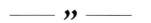

> *When auditioning children for the YPC, Núñez focused on finding the right attitude and strong parental support. "I'm looking for energy, enthusiasm, and I'm looking for a great parent who loves their child. Singing, we can teach anyone to sing," he explained. "We're not looking to create musicians. We're looking to create great people."*

With this goal in mind, Núñez took a job in 1988 with the Children's Aid Society, a charitable organization founded in 1853 to serve the needs of children in New York City, especially those from the poorest neighborhoods. Although he was basically hired as an afterschool counselor, he had ambitious plans from the start about using music to help the city's children. In 1990, he was given permission by the Society to organize a chorus that would bring together kids between the ages of 12 and 18 from diverse New York neighborhoods to learn and practice music.

There were rough spots to struggle through during the first years of the Children's Aid Chorus. Núñez had to work hard to recruit kids to commit to the program, and there wasn't much support from parents. The students who were involved had little or no knowledge of music, so they had to start with the most basic lessons. When looking for candidates for his program, though, Núñez was always much more concerned with their attitude and interest than in any musical knowledge or raw talent they might have.

Within a few years, the Children's Aid Chorus was achieving great success. The group worked hard, giving numerous performances around the city. By 1997 they had progressed to the point of traveling to Europe to take part in the Prague International Choir Festival and Competition. Just getting to the festival was a challenge, as the cost of the trip came to $1,700 for each child, an expense very few of their families could afford. The group needed to raise about $60,000 to make the trip a reality for the entire chorus. Undaunted, Núñez arranged a series of benefit concerts that successfully raised the needed funds. At the festival, they performed "Ave Maria," by Johannes Brahms, and Stephen Hatfield's "Nukapianguaq," a piece based on chants of the Inuit people. When they returned to New York, they brought home the competition's second-place silver trophy.

CAREER HIGHLIGHTS

Young People's Chorus of New York

When Núñez first started working as the director of music for the Children's Aid Society, he thought he would only do the job for a short while, then move on to some other sort of conducting work. Instead, he stayed in the position for nine years, inspired by his young students and their willingness to "work so hard and sing with such intensity."

Núñez left the Children's Aid Society to develop his dream of a citywide chorus for New York children. The program that had begun as the Children's Aid Chorus was transformed into the Young People's Chorus of New York, commonly known as the YPC. Money to run the program would come from tuition, private donations, and grants from foundations and corporations. Scholarships would be made available to any participant whose family could not afford the tuition. The main chorus would continue to be made up of children between the ages of 12 and 18, but junior choruses for younger children would also be formed. They would begin their first season by performing at some of the city's most famous landmarks, including St. Patrick's Cathedral and Rockefeller Center.

When Núñez had started the Children's Aid Chorus, he had to coax students to make a commitment to it. By the time he formed the YPC, he attracted so many hopeful kids to auditions that only about 1 in 10 could be chosen. A high level of musicianship was part of the overall goal, but when auditioning children, Núñez continued to focus more on finding the right attitude and strong parental support rather than any special talent. "I'm looking for energy, enthusiasm, and I'm looking for a great parent who loves their child. Singing, we can teach anyone to sing," he explained. "We're not looking to create musicians. We're looking to create great people."

Núñez hoped to do that by several means: using music as a vehicle to teach children to be disciplined and focused; helping them develop self-confidence and self-esteem through the mastery of difficult music; and

Núñez conducting a YPC concert at St. Patrick's Cathedral in New York City, 2010.

providing opportunities to make new connections in the world. "Once they are with us, they make better decisions; it impacts their schoolwork, and it encourages them to seek out a diverse community," Núñez observed. He took his concern for his students to a very personal level, regularly asking them how things were going at home, if they were keeping up with homework, or if they needed help or letters of recommendation as they began applying for admission to colleges.

The YPC grew rapidly, with divisions added for younger children and satellite programs started in several New York schools. As of 2011, there were more than 1,100 children involved in the YPC program. The vision of music as a means of cultural exchange is also reflected in the group's repertoire, which includes music drawn from many traditions, eras, and styles. The YPC maintains a busy schedule. The group gives regular performances at Carnegie Hall and serves as the resident choir for the Frederick P. Rose Hall at the Lincoln Center, as well as the Radio Choir for New York radio station WNYC. They have traveled to Asia, South America, and Europe to perform at festivals and competitions. They are considered one of the finest youth choirs in the world.

The YPC has also served as a model for affiliated programs in Tenafly, New Jersey, and Erie, Pennsylvania. Núñez has even reached out to bring his vision to the Dominican Republic, where he organized the National Children's Choir of Santo Domingo. As with the YPC, this choir seeks out children in the poorest neighborhoods. "If you go to the richest schools, you will get more money and be able to hire great people," he said, "But I want to bring the rich and poor together, as we did here. We already created one choir in a gang-run neighborhood, deep in the drug trade. I needed an armed escort. But I believe that music has the power to change society."

"Transient Glory"

In working with children, Núñez wanted both to change their lives and to change something about the world of choral music. Traditionally, the best contemporary composers have not written work intended for children's choruses. It was not seen as an area of serious music. Núñez set out to change that. Part of his plan was to use the YPC to demonstrate that a youth choir could indeed perform very complex, difficult music—and do it with technical excellence. He hoped the YPC would inspire composers to write works that were meant to utilize the unique sound of a youth choir. This would have the added benefit of increasing the selection of works available for youth choruses everywhere to perform.

Núñez called his ambitious project "Transient Glory." He explained the project like this: "transient because it's during a time of a child's voice when it's just before he becomes an adult, and glory because it's a glorious music." In 2001, his friend Ned Rorem, a composer, was hosting a concert of new music. Núñez persuaded Rorem to add the YPC to the concert lineup, and he also convinced four other respected composers to write pieces especially for the youth chorus. The YPC performed original works by Michael Torke, John Tavener, Elena Catch Turnen, and Nora Cora Rosenbaum. This was the beginning of a continuing series of Transient Glory concerts featuring new works by modern composers. "From there it just took off and we started doing concerts each year," Núñez remarked. "But what it did was, it put the children on the map of new music, real music. Even the *New York Times* started to critique it and that was what was unique."

In addition to commissioning new compositions from composers and performing them in concert, the Transient Glory project also involved creating recordings of this music and publishing it. The Transient Glory imprint was created at Boosey & Hawkes, the music publisher where Núñez is an editor. Works were commissioned yearly for concerts and recordings. David Del Tredici, Paquito D'Rivera, Dominick Argento, and Michael Nyman are just a few of the many respected composers who have contributed to the Transient Glory project. "What's unique about this," Núñez commented,

The first CD from the "Transient Glory" project.

"is that composers are studying this instrument [the children's choir] and taking advantage of what this instrument can do."Thanks to his efforts, the YPC has given performances of more than 60 new works in the Transient Glory series as of early 2012.

Núñez certainly had a part in inspiring composers with the warm, rich, expressive sound he has been able to create with the YPC. Reviewing the *Transient Glory* CD in the *American Record Guide,* Lindsay Koob wrote, "The singing of these gifted young folks (predominantly girls, as usual in America) simply blew me away! There are many competent and seasoned adult ensembles out there that would be hard-pressed to match this group's intonation, rhythmic precision, and enthusiastic confidence in these often very tricky pieces." A *New York Times* reviewer commenting on the recording *Transient Glory II* also praised the group: "These young singers are notable for the beauty of their youthfully pure voices and for their technical sophistication."

Awarded the MacArthur "Genius Grant"

In November 2011, Núñez was honored with a grant from the John D. and Catherine T. MacArthur Foundation. Individuals awarded MacArthur grants are given $500,000 over the course of five years to be used in any way they see fit to further their visions. Those selected for the award are typically people of such outstanding talent that it has earned the nickname the "Genius Grant." Upon learning that he was to be honored with a MacArthur grant, Núñez was naturally very pleased—with both the honor of winning the award and with the opportunities it would provide. "I feel that more than the money, the award itself, the title, is going to help me leverage being able to figure new things to do," he explained. "I feel like there is a spotlight that's been placed on the Young People's Chorus, on me, and the choruses all over the country, actually. And we have to do something for the society and to build communities. You know, using the child voice as a way of reaching out to each other."

Work with the YPC keeps Núñez very busy, but he makes it a point to find time to continue his involvement in other aspects of music. He composes music that is noted for its original arrangements and the frequent use of Latin rhythms and melodies. His works include classical pieces for solo instruments, large choruses, and orchestras. From 2003 to 2010, he served as the director of choral activities at New York University. He travels the country working as a guest conductor and a teacher for workshops held at universities and music societies. He works as an advisor and editor at the Boosey & Hawkes music publishing company. He also serves as the conductor for the University Glee Club of New York, a 120-person, elite men's choir that was originally formed in 1894 and has had only had five conductors since then. He has served as the music advisor to the General Consul of the Dominican Republic in New York, and in November 2011, he was given an award from the Dominican Republic for his work with the children of that country. Shortly after, he was also invited to the White

> *Funding for arts education is one of the first things to be eliminated when school budgets are cut, according to Núñez. "All the entertainment that we see is about singing and the arts," he said. "Yet, in schools, there is less and less of it being offered, especially to children of less social economic means. So how do we balance that?"*

Núñez and the YPC share their joy in music.

House in Washington DC, where he was presented with a National Arts and Humanities Youth Program Award by First Lady Michelle Obama.

Núñez points out that funding for arts education is frequently one of the first things to be eliminated when schools are forced to cut their budgets. "It's unfortunate," he said. "All the entertainment that we see is about singing and the arts.... Yet, in schools, there is less and less of it being offered, especially to children of less social economic means. So how do we balance that?" He believes that it is vital to find ways to do so because music can be such an important catalyst in children's lives, especially for children from disadvantaged backgrounds. And that's equally true for the children in the YPC. "These children, when they hear the applause that [is] not from their parents, but from a general audience of music lovers, people who know music and the applause is so strong. They say, you know what, I've contributed to society and I feel fabulous about myself."

HOME AND FAMILY

In 1993, Núñez married Dianne P. Berkun, who was the director of music at the Brooklyn Friends School, as well as the founder and director of the Brooklyn Youth Chorus. She continues to direct the Brooklyn Youth Chorus and is also the director of one of YPC's junior choruses. She and Núñez have one child, a son named Sebastian, born in 2007. Their marriage has ended.

SELECTED COMPOSITIONS

"Misa Pequeña"
"What Grandpa Told the Children"
"Cantan"
"Canticle: In Remembrance"
"The Sun Says His Prayers"
"Three Dominican Folk Songs"
"Your Heart Goes with Me"

HONORS AND AWARDS

Young Virtuosos International Composition grant
Man of Achievement (*Hispanic* magazine): 2005
One of the 100 most influential Hispanics (*Hispanic Business* magazine): 2005
ASCAP Concert Music Award: 2009
Man of the Year (La Sociedad Coral Latinoamericana): 2009
Choral Excellence Award (New York Choral Society): 2009
Award from the Dominican Republic: 2011
National Arts and Humanities Youth Program Award: 2011
MacArthur Fellowship: 2011

FURTHER READINGS

Periodicals

American Record Guide, Mar. 1, 2004, p.248
Brooklyn Daily Eagle, Aug. 18, 2009
Choir & Organ, Nov.-Dec., 2003, p.38
Latina Magazine, July 2003
New York Times, Apr. 24, 2003; Dec. 13, 2009; Oct. 4, 2011; Jan. 3, 2012, p.E1

Online Articles

nieonline.com/cvaonline/blog
(Classical Voice America Network, "The Kids Are All Right: Young People's Chorus of New York City at 92nd St. Y," May 9, 2011)
www.huffingtonpost.com
(Huffington Post, "More Music Please," Feb. 7, 2012)

www.pbs.org/newshour/art/blog
  (PBS, Art Beat, "Conversation: Francisco Núñez, Choral Conductor for
  Kids,"Sep. 23, 2011)
online.wsj.com
  (Wall Street Journal, "The Power to Foster Social Renewal through
  Song,"Dec. 15, 2011)

ADDRESS

Francisco J. Núñez
Young People's Chorus of NewYork City
1995 Broadway, Suite 305
NewYork, NY 10023

WEB SITES

franciscojnunez.com
www.ypc.org/aboutypc/fnunez.html

Justin Verlander 1983-

American Professional Baseball Pitcher for the
Detroit Tigers
Winner of the 2011 American League Most Valuable
Player Award and the Cy Young Award

BIRTH

Justin Brooks Verlander was born on February 20, 1983, in
Manakin Sabot, Virginia. His father, Richard Verlander, worked
as a pole climber for a telecommunications company and later
served as president of a local labor union. His mother, Kathy
Verlander, stayed home to care for Justin and his brother, Ben,
who is nine years younger.

YOUTH

Justin grew up on the outskirts of Richmond, Virginia, in what he once described as "a small, everybody-knows-everybody town." He always enjoyed playing sports, especially baseball, and developed a strong throwing arm at an early age. Unfortunately for his opponents, though, young Justin pitched with great velocity and terrible accuracy. "I started pitching when I was seven or eight," he remembered. "In Little League, I walked a lot of hitters, and I hit a ton of kids. They were all totally an accident. A couple of kids quit because I hit them a few times. A few kids were crying on deck before they faced me. They knew I might hit them in the head or something."

> "I started pitching when I was seven or eight," Verlander remembered. "In Little League, I walked a lot of hitters, and I hit a ton of kids. They were all totally an accident. A couple of kids quit because I hit them a few times. A few kids were crying on deck before they faced me. They knew I might hit them in the head or something."

By the time he was 13, Justin was so overpowering as a pitcher that his father no longer felt safe catching for him. His parents sent him to train at the Richmond Baseball Academy, which was run by former Major League Baseball (MLB) scout Bob Smith. As Justin's pitching skills continued to improve, the Verlanders also made sure that their son did not become arrogant. At one game, Justin recalled, "some parent asked me if I was any good, and I said, 'Yeah, I'm the best.' And my parents told me I couldn't be like that, that I had to be humble. That stuck with me."

EDUCATION

By the time he began pitching for Goochland High School, Verlander had fixed his accuracy problem. He struck out 144 batters in 72 innings and posted an incredible 0.38 earned run average or ERA (the average number of earned runs given up by a pitcher per nine innings pitched) during his high school career. Despite his outstanding statistics and a fastball clocked at 93 miles per hour, however, he was passed over for the MLB draft. "Senior year of high school I had strep, and I came out on opening day when all the scouts were there," he explained. "I was throwing 83 when I was supposed to be throwing 93. By the time I got [my pitching speed] back up there [later in] the season, no one was there to see it."

After graduating from high school in 2002, Verlander accepted an athletic scholarship to attend Old Dominion University in Norfolk, Virginia. He was the star pitcher on the school's baseball team for three seasons, compiling a 21-18 win-loss record and striking out 427 batters in 335 2/3 innings. Over the course of his college career, Verlander added 15 pounds to his lanky, 6-foot-5-inch frame, pushed the speed of his fastball to over 100 miles per hour, and started developing tricky changeup and curveball pitches. By the time he left Old Dominion in 2004, without completing his degree in communications, Verlander was considered one of the nation's top baseball prospects.

CAREER HIGHLIGHTS

Major League Baseball—The Detroit Tigers

Verlander was selected second overall in the 2004 MLB amateur draft by the Detroit Tigers, a historic franchise that had set a new American League (AL) record by losing 119 games in 2003. He signed a contract with the team that October that included a $3.12 million signing bonus.

After becoming a millionaire at age 21, Verlander could afford to pay up on a deal he had negotiated with a friend back in tenth grade. "I wanted a chocolate milk that cost 50 cents, and I didn't have the money," he remembered. "So I said, 'How about I give you 1 percent of my signing bonus if you give me 50 cents now?' He found a napkin, wrote it up, and I signed it. I forgot about it, but after I signed [with the Tigers], he comes over and whips out this old napkin. I'm like, Oh my God! My bonus was three-point-something million. Was a chocolate milk worth $3,000? I want to say yes. I was parched."

Verlander launched his professional baseball career in 2005 at the Tigers' Class A minor-league affiliate in Lakeland, Florida. He posted a 9-2 record with an impressive 1.67 ERA and struck out 104 batters in 86 innings. His strong start earned him a promotion to the Tigers' Class AA affiliate in Erie, Pennsylvania, where he went 2-0 with a 0.28 ERA and struck out 32 batters in 32 innings. Verlander went on to be named a Minor League All-Star by *Baseball America* and Minor League Starting Pitcher of the Year by MLB.com. He was even called up to the big leagues to start two games for the Tigers that season. His first major-league appearance came on July 4, 2005, in a game the Tigers lost to the Cleveland Indians.

Winning Rookie of the Year Honors

While Verlander was working his way up through the minor leagues in 2005, the big-league Tigers posted a disappointing 71-91 record. Team

Verlander throwing during batting practice for the first time in spring training in Lakeland, Florida, while still in the minor leagues, 2005.

owner Mike Ilitch fired manager Alan Trammell and replaced him with veteran manager Jim Leyland. During spring training for the 2006 MLB season, Leyland was so impressed by Verlander that he added him to the Tigers' roster as the team's fifth starter. Verlander joined a promising rotation that included up-and-coming young pitchers Nate Robertson and Jeremy Bonderman, veteran Kenny Rogers, and reliever Joel Zumaya.

To the amazement of many baseball fans, the rookie emerged as the best of the bunch. Verlander notched 10 victories by midseason and barely missed earning a spot on the All-Star Team. He finished the year with the fourth-best record in the American League at 17-9, and he added a solid 3.63 ERA and 124 strikeouts in 186 innings. Verlander's impressive debut helped the Tigers clinch a playoff spot with a 95-67 record. The team went on to beat the New York Yankees 3 games to 1 in the best-of-5 AL Division Series, then swept the Oakland Athletics 4-0 in the best-of-7 AL Championship Series. Verlander started and won Game 2 in both series.

Detroit then advanced to the World Series for the first time in 22 years, where the Tigers faced the St. Louis Cardinals. Game 1 featured a showdown between two rookie pitchers, Verlander and the Cards' Anthony Reyes. While Reyes shut down the Tigers' bats, Verlander's outing was ruined by a series of defensive lapses, and the Tigers lost the game 7-2. Verlander took the mound again in Game 5, with the Tigers down 3 games to 1 and facing elimination. He made a throwing error in the fourth inning that led to a St. Louis rally. The Tigers lost the game 4-2 and were knocked out of the World Series. Still, Verlander insisted that he had enjoyed the experience. "This has been nothing but fun, getting to know these guys and getting to be a part of this team. I couldn't ask for more in my rookie year," he declared. "The total end result, I would change a little bit. But in the long scheme of things, excluding this, I wouldn't change a thing. This has been an unbelievable run."

Despite the disappointing result of the World Series, Verlander's rookie season was a tremendous success. He

> **"**
>
> *"This has been nothing but fun, getting to know these guys and getting to be a part of this team. I couldn't ask for more in my rookie year,"* Verlander declared. *"The total end result, I would change a little bit. But in the long scheme of things, excluding this, I wouldn't change a thing. This has been an unbelievable run."*
>
> **"**

*Verlander pitching during Game 1 of the World Series,
October 2006—his rookie season.*

won the AL Rookie of the Year Award in a landslide, earning 26 of 28 first-place votes and 133 points. Verlander was outside washing his car when members of the team called to tell him he had received what he called "the ultimate honor." "I was pretty excited, but I had to go out and finish washing my car—can't leave the soap on there," he joked.

Over the course of his rookie season, Verlander impressed many people with his attitude as well as his talent. "He can hit triple digits with his fastball, has a very good changeup and curveball, and can throw all three for strikes," said teammate Nate Robertson. "No hitter I've ever talked with wants to face stuff like that. Plus he's receptive, wants to learn, and works hard. If he can keep doing this, especially when he hits valleys, he's going to be special."

Still, some observers expressed concerns about the extent to which the Tigers relied upon Verlander's young arm. They worried that fatigue from the long season might result in an injury that could threaten his promising career. After all, Verlander pitched 77 more innings in 2006 than he had in 2005; many experts recommend that young pitchers only increase their total innings by about 30 per year. Critics noted that Verlander's performance declined toward the end of the regular season, when he lost 5 of his final 8 decisions.

Verlander admitted that he suffered some physical effects of overwork, but he claimed that the experience helped him learn how to better condition his body for the demands of an MLB season. "After a start, the next day I'm real sore. I feel like crap. It's a weird feeling. You're tired, and your shoulder feels sore, dull," he related. "I'd say from about the halfway point, it was all downhill. It was a battle. It was a blessing in disguise. I'm lucky I didn't get hurt, but I went into that offseason and I knew what I needed to do."

Coming into His Own

Verlander's hard training during the offseason paid off in 2007. He started off his second MLB season by throwing his first career no-hitter against the Milwaukee Brewers on June 12, 2007. Determined to avoid interfering with Verlander's concentration as the young ace retired batter after batter, Tigers catcher Ivan (Pudge) Rodriguez made a point of not going out to the mound to talk to him during the game. "I didn't talk to him, I just left him alone," Rodriguez remembered. "Then, in the ninth inning, he tried to come over and talk to me and I told him, 'You know what? Go away. Just do what you've been doing. You're fine. You don't have to change anything.'" Verlander later claimed that his no-hitter had been inspired by his younger brother,

Verlander posing with fans after his first no-hitter, 2007.

who had pitched a no-hit high school game a few weeks earlier. "My parents called to tell me," he noted. "I'm the older brother, so I had to top him."

Verlander went on to post a stellar 18-6 record in 2007. His win total ranked sixth in the American League. He also struck out 183 batters in 201 2/3 innings with a 3.66 ERA, which helped him earn his first appearance in the MLB All-Star Game. Verlander's strong performance was not enough to take the Tigers back to the World Series, however. The team finished the year with an 88-74 record and missed the playoffs.

The 2008 season turned out to be a rough one for both Verlander and his team. Verlander's record dropped to 11-17, while his ERA increased to 4.84. He struck out 20 fewer batters than the year before (163) and walked 20 more (87), while pitching the same number of innings. He blamed his struggles on mechanical problems with his pitching motion as well as mental fatigue. "For two years, this game was easy," he acknowledged. "Just go out there and throw and—not that I wasn't giving it my all, because I was—win 17, win 18. Hey, what can go wrong? And then the next year, bam! Things catch

Verlander claimed that his first no-hitter was inspired by his younger brother, who had pitched a no-hit high school game a few weeks earlier. "My parents called to tell me," he noted. "I'm the older brother, so I had to top him."

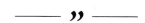

up with you. This game has a way of taking you down in a hurry. It was an eye-opener." Meanwhile, the Tigers posted a disappointing 74-88 record and finished fifth in their division.

Verlander returned to form in 2009 and turned in the best season of his young career. He went 19-9 with a 3.45 ERA and struck out 269 batters in 240 innings. He led all starting pitchers in the American League in victories, strikeouts, and innings pitched. His strong performance helped him earn a second selection to the All-Star Team and a third-place finish in voting for the Cy Young Award, which is presented annually to the best pitcher in each league.

Despite Verlander's contributions, the Tigers collapsed down the stretch and barely missed making the playoffs with a 86-77 record. "October was tough. You've got the whole season, then this huge letdown toward the very end. I had never experienced anything like that," Verlander stated. "We had the team. To be honest with you, man, I wish we could go back and have another chance to make those playoffs. I believe we matched up well against anybody."

During the offseason, Verlander signed a five-year, $80-million contract extension with the Tigers that made him one of the highest-paid pitchers in the game. He had another outstanding year in 2010, posting the fourth-best record in the league at 18-9 and lowering his ERA to 3.37. He also struck out 219 batters in 224 1/3 innings and made his third appearance in the All-Star Game. The Tigers' record dropped to 81-81 despite Verlander's stellar showing, however, and the team failed to make the playoffs once again.

Becoming the Best

From the outset, the 2011 season showed signs of being a very special one for Verlander. He notched his 1,000th career strikeout in April against the Chicago White Sox. Then, on May 7, he threw his second career no-hitter against the Toronto Blue Jays. Verlander dominated that game so completely that he was one eighth-inning walk away from pitching a perfect game (allowing no runners on base). He also maintained his velocity throughout the game, throwing a 100 mile-per-hour fastball to the very last batter. The whole experience gave him a tremendous boost in confidence. "I had a different feeling in that game," he recalled. "I just felt very calm and relaxed. And I remember thinking, 'Let's try to carry this over for the rest of the season.'"

Verlander's confidence showed every time he took the mound in 2011, and he came tantalizingly close to no-hitters on several other occasions. "In the past I've gotten away with my stuff and making a lot of mistakes. This year I feel like I've just found myself to be more mentally prepared and physically prepared," he explained. "It's hard for me to put a finger on what I know, but it's there. Time. Experience of pitching at this level for a while now. You log it all away, and it opens up a new game to you, almost."

By midseason, baseball analysts agreed that Verlander had brought his game to a new level, and many argued that he was the best pitcher in baseball. He showed more maturity on the mound, trusting his ability to make pitches and not letting an occasional mistake bother him. Although the average speed of his fastball (95.3 miles per hour) remained the highest of any MLB pitcher, he mixed in more off-speed pitches. By pacing himself, he was often able to throw progressively faster pitches as games wore on. "There were times early in his career when he would overthrow," said Tigers General Manager Dave Dombrowski. "He realizes now that throwing harder

Teammates rush out as Verlander and Detroit Tigers catcher Alex Avila celebrate another no-hitter, May 2011.

isn't always the solution. If you can throw 93 to 95 on the outside corner enough and you have a plus curve and a plus changeup, that's pretty good. Of course, when you dial it up to 100 when you need it, that's good too."

By the end of the 2011 season, Verlander led the league in nearly every statistical category for pitchers. He posted the best record at 24-5, the lowest ERA at 2.40, the most strikeouts at 250, and the most innings pitched at 251. He became only the 11th pitcher in the American League ever to win the elusive "triple crown" by leading in victories, ERA, and strikeouts in the same season. Verlander's incredible season earned him a slew of awards. He made the All-Star Team for the fourth time, was named *Baseball Digest* Pitcher of the Year and MLB Players' Choice Player of the Year, and won the Cy Young Award as the best pitcher in the American League by a unanimous vote.

Claiming the Most Valuable Player Award

Many baseball analysts and Tigers fans also considered Verlander a leading candidate for the American League's Most Valuable Player (MVP) Award. No one doubted that he played a vital role in the Tigers' success, as the team posted a 95-67 record for the season and won the AL Central Division. Yet some people argued that the MVP award should go to a player who took the field every day, rather than a pitcher who only appeared in one out of every four or five games. For this reason, the last starting pitcher to claim the MVP award was Roger Clemens in 1986. Verlander believed that he deserved as much consideration for the award as any other player. "Pitchers are players," he stated. "It's the Most Valuable Player Award." His supporters also pointed out that Verlander had faced 969 hitters during the 2011 season, while Boston Red Sox outfielder Jacoby Ellsbury—also considered a leading MVP candidate—had only appeared at the plate 729 times.

The MVP debate continued throughout the playoffs, as the Tigers beat the New York Yankees 3 games to 2 in the AL Division Series. Verlander started Game 1 against Yankees ace C.C. Sabathia, but the highly anticipated pitchers' duel never materialized. The game was postponed due to heavy rain after two innings with the score tied 1-1. When the game resumed the next day, neither pitcher returned to the mound, and the Tigers lost 9-3. Verlander faced Sabathia once again in Game 3. He pitched 8 innings, allowed 4 runs, and struck out 11 batters, as the Tigers won the game 5-4.

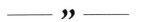

"I love the Tigers. The fans there have seen me grow up not only as a person but as a player. I feel a sense of belonging there, and I think the fans feel that connection as well."

In the AL Championship Series, the Tigers lost to the powerful Texas Rangers 4 games to 2. Verlander started Game 1 against Texas, but lengthy rain delays limited his time on the mound to 4 innings. He allowed 3 runs and took the loss as the Tigers went down by a score of 3-2. Verlander pitched again with his team facing elimination in Game 5. He went 7 innings, struck out 8 batters, and allowed 4 runs, but ended up winning the game 7-5. Unfortunately, Detroit was eliminated in Game 6 when the series returned to Texas. "Day in and day out, we go through it as a family," Verlander said afterward of his teammates. "To come up a bit short is tough."

Verlander's disappointment at missing a chance to pitch in the World Series was eased somewhat when he received the American League MVP Award. He thus became the 10th pitcher in history to win both the Cy Young and the MVP award in the same season, and only the second pitcher (after Don Newcombe) ever to have won both of those awards as well as Rookie of the Year honors. Verlander was proud to claim the MVP trophy on behalf of all pitchers. "I think this set a precedent," he said. "I'm happy

Verlander pitching against the Texas Rangers in Game 5 of the 2011 American League Championship Series. The Tigers lost the series four games to two.

the voters acknowledged that we do have a major impact in this game and we can be extremely valuable to our team and its success."

By the end of the 2011 season, Verlander had posted a remarkable 107 career victories in only 6 full seasons in the majors. "He works hard and has the desire to be the best," said Tigers Manager Jim Leyland. "There is nobody I'd rather have on the mound in a must-win game." Even though Detroit did not quite reach the World Series, Verlander feels confident about his team's future chances. "I still think our owner and our management is going to put us in a position every year where we can win. That's one of the things I look at when I think about being in Detroit for a while. I'm an extremely competitive guy in everything I do, and I want to win at all costs," he noted. "I love the Tigers. The fans there have seen me grow up not only as a person but as a player. I feel a sense of belonging there, and I think the fans feel that connection as well."

HOME AND FAMILY

During the offseason, Verlander lives in a townhome on a golf course in Lakeland, Florida. His favorite room is his "man cave," where he plans to display his Cy Young and MVP trophies. "I have a humongous couch with a 12-foot TV projector and a Ping-Pong table," he said. "I guess I'm going to find some space for some hardware."

HOBBIES AND OTHER INTERESTS

In his free time, Verlander enjoys playing golf, watching movies, and playing video games. His all-time favorite movies are the baseball-related *Field of Dreams* and *The Rookie,* but he also likes the *Spiderman* series and other action movies. He was excited to be featured on the cover of the *Major League Baseball 2K12* video game. Verlander also hosts a weekly poker game and occasionally plays competitively in casinos. "I just like to have fun," he noted. "I like to hang out with the guys a lot and just live my life."

Verlander also participates in a number of charity functions with the Tigers, including the Tigers Dreams Come True Program, the Detroit Tigers Autographed Memorabilia Donation Program, the Tigers Winter Caravan, and the Children's Miracle Network.

HONORS AND AWARDS

Minor League All-Star (*Baseball America*): 2005
Minor League Starting Pitcher of the Year (MLB.com): 2005
American League Rookie of the Year Award: 2006

American League All-Star Team: 2007, 2009, 2010, 2011
American League Cy Young Award: 2011
American League Most Valuable Player Award: 2011
Pitcher of the Year (*Baseball Digest*): 2011
MLB Players' Choice Player of the Year: 2011

FURTHER READING

Periodicals

Baseball Digest, Sep. 2006, p.60; May 2007, p.56; Jan.-Feb. 2012, p.22
New York Times, Sep. 18, 2009; Nov. 22, 2011
Sporting News, Mar. 15, 2010, p.52; Sep. 12, 2011, p.36
Sports Illustrated, Aug. 28, 2006, p.50; May 28, 2007, p.14; Sep. 19, 2011, p.62
Sports Illustrated Kids, Aug. 2011, p.18
USA Today, June 26, 2006; June 20, 2007; July 8, 2011; Oct. 5, 2011; Nov. 16, 2011

Online Articles

www.baseball-reference.com/bullpen/Justin%20Verlander
   (Baseball Reference, "Justin Verlander," no date)
www.mensjournal.com/justin-verlander
   (Men's Journal, "Shut Up and Throw the Ball," Apr. 16, 2012)
sportsillustrated.cnn.com/2012/writers/joe_lemire/05/02/justin.verlander
   .velocity/
   (Sports Illustrated, "How Justin Verlander Is Defying Conventional Wisdom," May 2, 2012)

ADDRESS

Justin Verlander
Detroit Tigers
Comerica Park
2100 Woodward Ave.
Detroit, MI 48201

WEB SITES

detroit.tigers.mlb.com
sportsillustrated.cnn.com/baseball/mlb/players/7590
espn.go.com/mlb/player/_/id/6341/justin-verlander

Florence Welch 1986-

British Singer and Musician
Lead Singer of Musical Group Florence + the
Machine

BIRTH

Florence Leontine Mary Welch was born on October 28, 1986, in Camberwell, a southern district of London, England. She was the oldest of three children born to Nick Welch, who worked in advertising, and Evelyn Welch, an American-born professor of art history and Renaissance studies. She has two younger siblings, Grace and John James.

YOUTH

Music was a big part of Welch's life when she was growing up. She joined her school choir and at 10 or 11 played the lead female role in a school production of the musical *Bugsy Malone.* Her father recalled that usually parents were only interested in watching their own children, "but when Florence sang, the whole audience was suddenly fully engaged. I remember thinking: 'Cripes, she's got a voice—this is serious.'" She also sang at various family funerals, including one for her grandfather Colin Welch, the noted satirist and newspaper editor. Although she did not play an instrument, she was already writing songs by the time she was 13. "My first songs were about imaginary break-ups," she recalled. "I'd never even had a boyfriend and it was all very flowery and poetic." She also had a fascination with dark and spooky things, including witches, vampires, werewolves, graveyards, and paintings of religious martyrs.

> *Welch was already writing songs by the time she was 13. "My first songs were about imaginary break-ups," she recalled. "I'd never even had a boyfriend and it was all very flowery and poetic."*

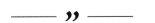

Welch was 13 when her parents divorced. Soon after, her mother married a widowed neighbor and the two families moved in together. With three older stepsiblings in the mix, there was a lot of tension in the house. (She also gained a fourth stepsibling when her father remarried.) With all the family drama, Welch rebelled. She stayed out late at parties held in abandoned buildings, where she learned to sing loudly to cut through the noise. As she grew older, her lyrics also grew darker. "I've always been attracted to dark imagery," she noted. "I used to believe in vampires and werewolves. I get night terrors, panic attacks. Even as a kid, I'd be more inclined to write about a flower dying than blossoming." She formed a band called the Toxic Cockroaches with a schoolmate and also took voice lessons. "It was too constraining for me," she recalled. "When I was told to preserve my voice by not partying or talking loudly, I thought, WRONG GIRL. There was no freedom for me in singing classically."

EDUCATION

Welch completed her secondary education at Alleyn's School, a private school in Dulwich, southeast London. She was diagnosed with dyslexia, a reading disability, and dysmetria, a problem judging distances, but she still

Welch has become known for her creative approach to costumes for all her shows.

earned good grades. In high school in Great Britain, students study specific subjects for their last two years and then take tests in order to qualify for college. Welch earned A-levels (Advanced Level) in several subjects, including art, English, and history. She entered the Camberwell College of Arts, part of the University of the Arts London. She planned to study illustration, but instead much of her work tended towards installations and performance art. She famously created a six-foot piece making fun of herself in fake flowers. She was more focused on college bands than college classes, however, and left after 18 months to focus on her music career.

CAREER HIGHLIGHTS

Breaking into the Music Business

Welch was 19 when she and her band signed a contract with a music manager. It wasn't a good match, and when she discovered she could get out of the contract by resigning from the band, she left the group. "I just didn't have a nice time," she recalled. "I didn't play an instrument, so I always thought I had to be a singer in a band ... then I found the drums." She sang on and off at area clubs until she found her manager, DJ-promoter Mairead Nash, by singing to her in a nightclub ladies' room. With a friend, keyboard player and producer Isabella Summers, Welch began writing songs and putting together demo recordings. They nicknamed each other "Florence Robot" and "Isabella Machine." When Welch began performing their songs live, she shortened "Florence Robot/Isa Machine" to Florence + the Machine. The name stuck, even though the line-up of musicians who formed "the Machine" has rotated and changed since then.

Welch spent the next two years experimenting with musical styles and seeking the right record company. "I used to make 10-minute songs about stationery and dead swans," she recalled. "I felt like a bit of a fraud when the record companies were taking me out for dinner. I didn't actually know what I could offer them, and I felt they had a certain idea of what they wanted me to be." By 2008, she signed with a record label, Island Records, that was willing to let her make music the way she wanted. She wrote lyrics inspired by "that feeling you get when you wake up in the morning with that creeping unknown dread that follows you around all day." Her songs often transposed lyrical images with strong percussion to create music that was both primal and thoughtful. Welch added another unique sound to her group when a harpist walked by the studio where she was working one day. "We figured why not get him in to actually play it," she remembered, "and it sounded so great that we just decided to use it on

Lungs *was Florence + the Machine's debut album.*

everything." In the summer of 2008 the group toured Europe in a camper van, opening for American electronic rock group MGMT.

In June 2008 Florence + the Machine released their first single, "Kiss with a Fist." Welch wrote the song when she was 17, using images of physical violence to portray the extreme feeling of young love. The song hit the British charts and the group performed it on British television. Welch had not even completed an album when she got her first major recognition. In February 2009 she received the BRIT Awards' Critics' Choice prize for the British artist most likely to break through in the coming year. Soon after, she and songwriting partner Isa Summers began writing a song by banging on studio walls with their hands. The result was "Dog Days Are Over," the group's next single and a worldwide breakout hit. "I said to Isa: 'This is it, this is what I want to do,'" Welch recalled. "That song represents the whole album coming together for me."

In July 2009 Florence + the Machine released their first album, *Lungs,* in the United Kingdom. It debuted at No. 2 on the British charts—kept out of the top spot only by the recently deceased Michael Jackson—and stayed on the charts for 28 weeks before finally hitting No. 1. The artist described her sound as "choral, gospel, chamber pop with heavy tribal drum stylings," and it was further distinguished by her powerful voice. That year *Lungs* was nominated for the Mercury Music Prize, a prestigious award for the year's best album voted on by British musicians and industry insiders. In 2010, *Lungs* won the Brit Award for album of the year. "That was a big moment for us," Welch noted. "You don't create music to win awards, but it is very nice when it happens."

Finding an American Audience

In October 2009 *Lungs* was released in the United States. Over the next year, songs from the album were all over American radio and television. "Dog Days Are Over" hit No. 21 on *Billboard*'s Hot 100 chart and was covered on the popular musical television show "Glee." Other Florence + the Machine songs appeared on the American TV shows "Grey's Anatomy," "Community," "90210," and "Gossip Girl"; Welch even performed on an episode of the latter show. Another song from the album, "Heavy in Your Arms," was chosen for the soundtrack to the popular 2010 film *The Twilight Saga: Eclipse.* By the end of 2010, *Lungs* had hit No. 2 on *Billboard*'s Alternative Album chart and No. 1 on their Heatseekers Albums chart for new and developing acts.

Welch made an impression on audiences through live performances as well, especially her appearance at the 2010 MTV Music Awards, where she had been nominated for Video of the Year and Best Rock Video. Her stage appearance, during which she rose from lying on a rotating platform to belt out "Dog Days Are Over," was the talk of the evening. The singer reflected on her ability to become larger-than-life on stage and attributed it to watching her mother, an art professor. "She's not a performer," Welch explained. "But when she gets on stage to give a lecture she becomes this heightened version of herself. She can suddenly hold the whole room rapt. I think that's where it comes from." For Welch, performing was a way to express her deepest, most heart-felt emotions. "You can feel things violently. It's a beautiful word. I'm such a non-violent person, too. I keep so much inside. I'm the least aggressive person ever. I can't argue. ... Music is my way out. I keep things locked up and never say anything."

Florence + the Machine opening a concert for U2 in Miami, Florida, 2011.

The year 2011 brought a lot of success for Welch and Florence + the Machine. The group began headlining their own U.S. shows, and they opened several U.S. concerts for the Irish rock group U2. Florence + the Machine was also nominated for the Grammy Award for Best New Artist. At the Grammys show, Welch performed live with star singers Yolanda Adams, Christina Aguilera, Jennifer Hudson, and Martina McBride in a tribute to the Queen of Soul, Aretha Franklin. By the end of 2011, *Lungs* had sold over 3.5 million copies worldwide.

By that point Welsh was ready to record her second album. Although she had offers to record with the hottest American producers in Los Angeles, she decided to remain in England and continue working with producer-songwriter Paul Epworth, noted for his work on British singer Adele's smash album *21*. The second Florence + the Machine album, *Ceremonials*, debuted in fall 2011. "I wanted it to be more dark, more heavy, bigger drum sounds, bigger bass, but with more of a whole sound," she said of the album. "So it sounded like a whole project rather than a scrapbook of ideas, which, for better or for worse, the first one was. That was a real specific thing: I wanted to work in one place with one producer." She also wanted to highlight the members of her band—synthesizer player Isa Summers, drummer Chris Hayden, harpist Tom Moth, guitarist Rob Ackroyd, pianist Rusty Bradshaw, and bass player Mark Saunders. "This time I

The Chanel fashion show at Paris Fashion Week, with Welch singing from inside a clam shell, October 2011.

really wanted to give the music space to breathe and for the band to be able to experiment." The album debuted at No. 6 on the *Billboard* album chart and earned Welch Brit Award nominations for album of the year and best female solo artist.

Becoming a Fashion Icon

In addition to her success in the music world, Welch soon became a favorite of fashion designers. Becoming a fashion icon was not something she would have foreseen. "I was a short, chubby kid," she remembered. "It wasn't until I was 17 that I really grew into myself and started wearing the clothes I wanted to wear." She experimented with vintage clothes, found glamorous gowns like those she had admired as a child, and had a stage of wearing Goth clothes, with "bat-wing costumes" and black lipstick. She tried many different hair colors before fixing on bright red, which set off her blue eyes and pale, porcelain skin. Style mavens appreciated her dramatic flair and fondness for using vintage clothing, including many pieces found at flea markets the day of her performances. "I didn't construct the image deliberately but as the music got more overpowering, I felt I needed to compete with it," she explained. "I wanted something that would put me in a more dramatic place and it just happened as I toured." Her costumes became an important part of her stage persona. "What I wear on stage really can affect my performance, from how I move to how I feel," she said. "When I'm on stage it's really part of my armor, it makes me feel connected to my home and to myself. Besides, dressing up is just fun. It makes life better."

By 2011, Welch had been embraced by many noted designers. She was invited to sit in the front row at fashion shows by Valentino and Givenchy, and Gucci designed several outfits for her 2011 tour. She performed at the Metropolitan Museum's Costume Institute Gala, which honored the late designer Alexander McQueen, singing for an audience filled with celebrities like Madonna, Jay-Z, and Paul McCartney. In fall 2011 designer Karl Lagerfeld, the lead designer for the Chanel fashion house, recruited her to sing at his Paris fashion week show, which she did from inside a giant clam shell. Even when Welch wore a couture gown to the Grammys

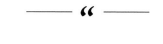

"I love singing, and I love playing music. So it's a real joy for me to get up there, and I'm grateful every time I step on the stage that I'm allowed to do it.

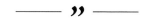

that some critics disliked, designers appreciated her daring. In response to the criticism, she said, "People can say a million bad things about wearing that Givenchy dress and I would not care! I was so lucky to have on something so beautiful that day. If you know yourself and you know what you like then don't worry about it." For the singer, music and fashion had become two different ways to express herself. "Music to me is so internal. It's physical and it's emotional," she explained. "Whereas fashion is so much about the external that it's almost like a break. It's not inner turmoil. It's total escapism."

Welch and her group continued their conquest of the music world in 2012. They made an appearance on the noted acoustic performance show "MTV Unplugged," and the subsequent album, also titled *MTV Unplugged,* hit the *Billboard* album chart. The show was part of a more mature image Welch was developing. "I think, now, I feel a bigger sense of responsibility to the fans. To the people who come to see me play." The show attempted to capture Welch's joy in live performance. "I think it's that sense of wanting to make people let go," she explained. "What I really like seeing from the stage is people having their own moments, when people are doing some performance of their own." Florence + the Machine headlined their own tour in 2012, appearing all across the United States, Australia, and Europe. They were also scheduled for several festival appearances, including a featured performance at Chicago's noted Lollapalooza festival.

Whether through her recordings or on stage, Welch hoped to transport her listeners to another place, a world of heightened emotion. She wanted her music to be "something overwhelming and all-encompassing that fills you up, and you're either going to explode with it, or you're just going to disappear." Performing allowed Welch to experience that heightened emotion, and to share it with her fans. "I'm just an emotional creature.... I want to make people feel something good. It's essential. You should lift people." Although her rise to the top of the music world was swift, she hoped for a long career as a musician, bringing pleasure to her listeners. "I love singing, and I love playing music. So it's a real joy for me to get up there, and I'm grateful every time I step on the stage that I'm allowed to do it."

HOME AND FAMILY

Welch has been so busy recording and touring that as of 2012 she had not had time to find her own place to live. She still lives with her mother, stepfather, and extended family in her childhood home in London, and while on tour she was often accompanied by her sister. She has said that some day she would like to settle down and have children, but "I love singing. So I wouldn't want to give it up. I just think, hopefully, I would be able to fit all that in. At some point."

FAVORITE MUSIC

Welch's first influences were Disney movie musicals, especially *The Little Mermaid*; as a young girl she also discovered her father's classic rock CDs, including the Smiths, the Velvet Underground, and especially Grace Slick of Jefferson Airplane. As a teenager, she got into the local garage-punk scene and enjoyed punk-influenced bands like Green Day and Hole. She also listened to a lot of classic soul music, particularly Etta James, Nina Simone, and Billie Holliday. She has also acknowledged the influence of British female singers like Kate Bush and Annie Lennox of the Eurythmics, to whom she has been compared. Her own music collection contains all different sorts of music, including popular songs by Beyoncé and rappers Jay-Z and Kanye West. The singer made this analogy about her musical tastes: "I can't just have one painting—I need to cover the wall in paintings. It's the same with music. I want to mix everything together to create more."

HOBBIES AND OTHER INTERESTS

Although she left art school early, Welch still enjoys drawing and sketching. She brings sketchbooks along with her on tour and has considered returning to school to finish her illustration degree. She's also involved in several charities, specifically charities for sick children and teens.

RECORDINGS

Lungs, 2009
Ceremonials, 2011
MTV Unplugged, 2012

HONORS AND AWARDS

BRIT Awards (British Phonographic Industry): 2009, Critics' Choice Award; 2010, MasterCard British Album of the Year, for *Lungs*

MTV Video Music Award: 2011, best art direction, for "Dog Days Are Over"

NME Awards (*NME* magazine): 2012 (two awards), Best Solo Artist and Best Track, for "Shake It Out"

FURTHER READING

Periodicals

Billboard, Oct. 8, 2011
Entertainment Weekly, Apr. 13, 2012
Evening Standard (London), Oct. 24, 2008, p.41
Flare, Jan. 2012, p.66
Glamour, Nov. 2010, p.218
Guardian (England), Oct. 29, 2011
Interview, June/July 2009, p.46; Oct. 2011, p.68
Mail on Sunday (London), July 26, 2009, p.6
Rolling Stone, Dec. 23, 2010, p.32; Nov. 10, 2011; Nov. 24, 2011, p.42; July 21, 2012
Sunday Times (London), Sep. 20, 2009, p.14; Feb. 19, 2012
Sydney Morning Herald (Australia), August 1, 2009, p.4
Teen Vogue, Oct. 2009, p.74
USA Today, Oct. 31, 2011

Online Articles

www.billboard.com
(Billboard, "Florence and the Machine," no date)

www.dailymail.co.uk
  (London Daily Mail, "Florence Welch:'I Was Awkward, Intense, and Ridiculously Self-Conscious,'"Apr. 30, 2011)
www.ew.com
  (Entertainment Weekly, "Florence Welch: The Soundtrack of My Life," Apr 13, 2012)
www.kidzworld.com
  (Kidz World, "Florence and the Machine Bio,"May 28, 2012)
www.npr.org
  (National Public Radio, "Florence and the Machine: From Delicate to Fierce,"Apr. 7, 2010)

ADDRESS

Florence Welch
FATM Fan Mail
PO Box 67541
London, EC2P 2GL
United Kingdom

WEB SITE

www.florenceandthemachine.net

Photo and Illustration Credits

Front Cover/Photos: Judy Blume: Steve Rice/Star Tribune/ZUMA Press/Newscom; Ellen DeGeneres: Â© Telepictures Productions/Photofest; Drake: © 2010 Jason Moore/ZUMA Press/Newscom; Justin Verlander: Marlin Levison/Minneapolis Star Tribune/MCT/Newscom.

Judy Blume/Photos: Courtesy Random House, Inc. Photo © Sigrid Estrada (p. 9); Romain Blanquart/Detroit Free Press/MCT/Newscom (p. 11); Book cover: ARE YOU THERE GOD? IT'S ME, MARGARET. By Judy Blume. Published in the U.S. by Ember (Random House, Inc., New York). All rights reserved. Text © 1970, copyright renewed 1988 by Judy Blume. Cover art © 2009 by Dana Edmunds/Jupiter Images. Cover design by Kenny Holcomb. (p. 14); Book cover: IT'S NOT THE END OF THE WORLD by Judy Blume. Published in the U.S. by Delacorte Press (Random House, Inc., New York). All rights reserved. Text © 1972, copyright renewed 2003 by Judy Blume. Cover art © 2009 by Laurence Mouton/Veer. Cover design by Kenny Holcomb. (p. 17); Book cover: STARRING SALLY J. FREEDMAN AS HERSELF by Judy Blume. Published by Yearling (Random House, Inc., New York). All rights reserved. Text © 1977 by Judy Blume. Cover art © 2004 by Susy Pilgrim-Waters. (p. 20); Audio book cover: OTHERWISE KNOWN AS SHEILA THE GREAT by Judy Blume. Published by Listening Library (Ⓟ 2000 Random House, Inc., New York). All rights reserved. Text © 1972 by Judy Blume. Cover illustration © Peter H. Reynolds. (p. 23); Book cover: FOREVER by Judy Blume. Published by Simon Pulse (Simon & Schuster, New York). All rights reserved. Text © 1975, copyright renewed 2003 by Judy Blume. Cover designed by Russell Gordon. Cover photograph © 2007 Jupiter Images. (p. 25); ZUMA Press/Newscom (p. 27).

Ellen DeGeneres/Photos: Noel Vasquez/Getty Images for Extra (p. 33); Photofest (p. 35); © Touchstone Television/Photofest (p. 37); © ABC/Photofest (p. 39); Official White House Photo by Chuck Kennedy (p. 41); Movie still: FINDING NEMO © Disney/Pixar. All rights reserved (p. 43).

Drake/Photos: ZUMA Press/Newscom (p. 47); © CTV Television Network/Photofest (p. 49); AP Photo/Chris Pizzello (p. 51); Dana Edelson/NBC/NBCU Photo Bank via Getty Images (p. 54); Album cover: TAKE CARE © 2012 Universal Republic/UMG. All rights reserved. (p. 56).

Kevin Durant/Photos: AP Photo/Alonzo Adams (p. 59); AP Photo/Denis Poroy (p. 62); Larry Smith/Icon SMI/Newscom (p. 64); Otto Greule, Jr./Getty Images (p. 67); Martin Levison/Minneapolis Star Tribune/MCT/Newscom (p. 69); Don Emmert/AFP/Getty Images/Newscom (p. 72); John G. Mabanglo/EPA/Landov (p. 74).

Zaha Hadid/Photos: Udo Hesse/akg-images/Newscom (p. 79); Christopher Pillitz/ Getty Images (p. 81); Vitra Company Fire Station by Zaha Hadid, Weil am Rhein, Germany, 10/04/2006. Author: en:User:Sandstein, a.k.a. User:TheBernFiles. http:// en.wikipedia.org/wiki/File:Vitra_fire_station,_full_view,_Zaha_Hadid.jpg (p. 83); The Contemporary Art Center, Cincinnati OH, 12/06/2006. Author: Lanskeith17 http:// en.wikipedia.org/wiki/File:Contemp_Art_Center.JPG (p. 85); View Pictures/ UIG via Getty Images (p. 87); The rear (riverside) view of the Glasgow Riverside Museum, 2/15/2012. Author: Bjmullan http://en.wikipedia.org/wiki/File:Riverside_Museum_ rear_view.JPG (p. 89); Graham Barclay/Bloomberg via Getty Images (p. 91).

Josh Hutcherson/Photos: Daniel Deme/EPA/Landov (p. 95); © Studio Ghibli/Walt Disney Pictures/Photofest (p. 97); Movie still: BRIDGE TO TERABITHIA © Buena Vista Home Entertainment, Inc. and Walden Media, LLC. All rights reserved. (p. 99); © New Line/Photofest. Photo by Sebastian Raymond (p. 101); Movie still: THE HUNGER GAMES © 2012 Lionsgate. Photo by Murray Close (pp. 103 & 104).

Jerry Mitchell/Photos: Courtesy of the John D. & Catherine T. MacArthur Foundation (p. 109); Photo by John Vachon, FSA/OWI Collection, Prints & Photographs Division, Library of Congress, LC-USF33-001112-M1 (p. 111, top); Rolls Press/Popper foto/Getty Images (p. 111, bottom); MPI/Getty Images (p. 115); Michael Ochs Archive/Getty Images (p. 116); AP Photo/Jeff Guenther (p. 117); AP Photo/File (p. 119); AP Photo/Hattiesburg American/Kim Harris-Guillory (p. 121); AP Photo/Jack Thornell (p. 123, top); AP Images/Rogelio Solis (p. 123, bottom); Courtesy of the John D. & Catherine T. MacArthur Foundation (p. 125).

Chloë Grace Moretz/Photos: Vera Anderson/WireImage (p. 129); © MGM/Dimension Films/Photofest (p. 131); Movie still: DIARY OF A WIMPY KID. Photo: Rob McEwan © 2010 Twentieth Century Fox Film Corporation. All rights reserved. DIARY OF A WIMPY KID®, WIMPY KID™ and the Greg Heffley design™ are trademarks of Wimpy Kid, Inc. All rights reserved. (p. 133); Movie still: HUGO © 2011 Paramount Pictures and GK Films. All rights reserved. (p. 135); © Warner Bros. Pictures/Photofest (p. 137).

Francisco J. Núñez/Photos: Courtesy of the John D. & Catherine T. MacArthur Foundation (pp. 141 & 143); Courtesy Young People's Chorus of New York City: http://www.ypc.org (p. 146); CD Cover: TRANSIENT GLORY ℗© Young Peoples Chorus of NYC. All rights reserved. Produced by Francisco Núñez. Distributed by Vital Records, Inc. (p. 148); Courtesy Francisco J. Núñez: http://franciscojnunez.com (p. 150).

Justin Verlander/Photos: Mark Cunningham/Detroit Tigers (p. 153); Charles W. Luzier/Reuters/Newscom (p. 156); Mark Cunningham/Detroit Tigers (pp. 158 & 160); AP Photo/The Canadian Press/Darren Calabrese (p. 163); Mark Cunningham/Detroit Tigers (p. 165).

Florence Welch/Photos: © 2012 Universal Republic/UMG. All rights reserved. Photo by Elaine Constantine (p. 169); Carmen Jaspersen/dpa/picture-alliance/Newscom (p. 171); Album cover: LUNGS/Florence & The Machine © 2011 Universal Republic/UMG. All rights reserved. (p. 173); Jeff Daly/PictureGroup via AP Images (p. 175); Rex Features via AP Images (p. 176).

Cumulative Names Index

This cumulative index includes the names of all individuals profiled in *Biography Today* since the debut of the series in 1992.

For cumulative general, places of birth, and birthday indexes, please see biographytoday.com.

185

For cumulative general, places of birth, and birthday indexes, please see biographytoday.com.

For cumulative general, places of birth, and birthday indexes, please see biographytoday.com.

For cumulative general, places of birth, and birthday indexes, please see biographytoday.com.

191

For cumulative general, places of birth, and birthday indexes, please see biographytoday.com.

For cumulative general, places of birth, and birthday indexes, please see biographytoday.com.

Biography Today

For ages 9 and above

General Series

Biography Today **General Series** includes a unique combination of current biographical profiles that teachers and librarians — and the readers themselves — tell us are most appealing. The **General Series** is available as a 3-issue subscription; hardcover annual cumulation; or subscription plus cumulation.

Within the **General Series**, your readers will find a variety of sketches about:

- Authors
- Musicians
- Political leaders
- Sports figures
- Movie actresses & actors
- Cartoonists
- Scientists
- Astronauts
- TV personalities
- and the movers & shakers in many other fields!

"*Biography Today* will be useful in elementary and middle school libraries and in public library children's collections where there is a need for biographies of current personalities. High schools serving reluctant readers may also want to consider a subscription."
— *Booklist,* American Library Association

"Highly recommended for the young adult audience. Readers will delight in the accessible, energetic, tell-all style; teachers, librarians, and parents will welcome the clever format [and] intelligent and informative text. It should prove especially useful in motivating 'reluctant' readers or literate nonreaders."
— *MultiCultural Review*

"Written in a friendly, almost chatty tone, the profiles offer quick, objective information. While coverage of current figures makes *Biography Today* a useful reference tool, an appealing format and wide scope make it a fun resource to browse."   — *School Library Journal*

"The best source for current information at a level kids can understand."
— Kelly Bryant, School Librarian, Carlton, OR

"Easy for kids to read. We love it! Don't want to be without it."
— Lynn McWhirter, School Librarian, Rockford, IL

ONE-YEAR SUBSCRIPTION
- 3 softcover issues, 6" x 9"
- Published in January, April, and September
- 1-year subscription, list price $66. **School and library price $64**
- 150 pages per issue
- 10 profiles per issue
- Contact sources for additional information
- Cumulative Names Index

HARDBOUND ANNUAL CUMULATION
- Sturdy 6" x 9" hardbound volume
- Published in December
- List price $73. **School and library price $66 per volume**
- 450 pages per volume
- 30 profiles — includes all profiles found in softcover issues for that calendar year
- Cumulative General Index, Places of Birth Index, and Birthday Index

SUBSCRIPTION AND CUMULATION COMBINATION
- $110 for 3 softcover issues plus the hardbound volume

For Cumulative General, Places of Birth, and Birthday Indexes, please see www.biographytoday.com.